Darwin's
TORTOISE

D1736788

Other books by Robin Stewart

Children's books
  Moonbird
  New Faces (CBC Book of the Year 1995)
  Wombat: Bush Babies Solo Series (CBC Notable Book 2003)
  Koala: Bush Babies Solo Series
  Alternative Pets
  Charles Darwin's Big Idea

Adult non-fiction books
  The Clean House Effect
  From Seeds to Leaves
  Envirocat
  Chemical Free Home
  Chemical Free Pest Control
  Chasing Rainbows
  The Dog Book
  Australian Green Home and Garden
  Tread Lightly

Darwin's
TORTOISE

Robin Stewart

Illustrated by Anna Crichton

THE AMAZING TRUE STORY OF HARRIET, THE WORLD'S OLDEST LIVING CREATURE

Black Inc.

Published by Black Inc.,
an imprint of Schwartz Publishing Pty Ltd
Level 5, 289 Flinders Lane
Melbourne Victoria 3000 Australia
email: enquiries@blackincbooks.com
http://www.blackincbooks.com

The National Library of Australia Cataloguing-in-Publication entry:

Stewart, Robin E. (Robin Elaine), 1943– .
Darwin's tortoise : the amazing true story of Harriet, the world's oldest living creature.

For children.
ISBN 1 86395 373 6.

1. Harriet (Tortoise) – Juvenile literature.
2. Galápagos tortoise – Juvenile literature.
I. Crichton, Anna.
II. Title.

597.9246

Book design: Gina Batzakis Design
Printed by: Imago

Contents

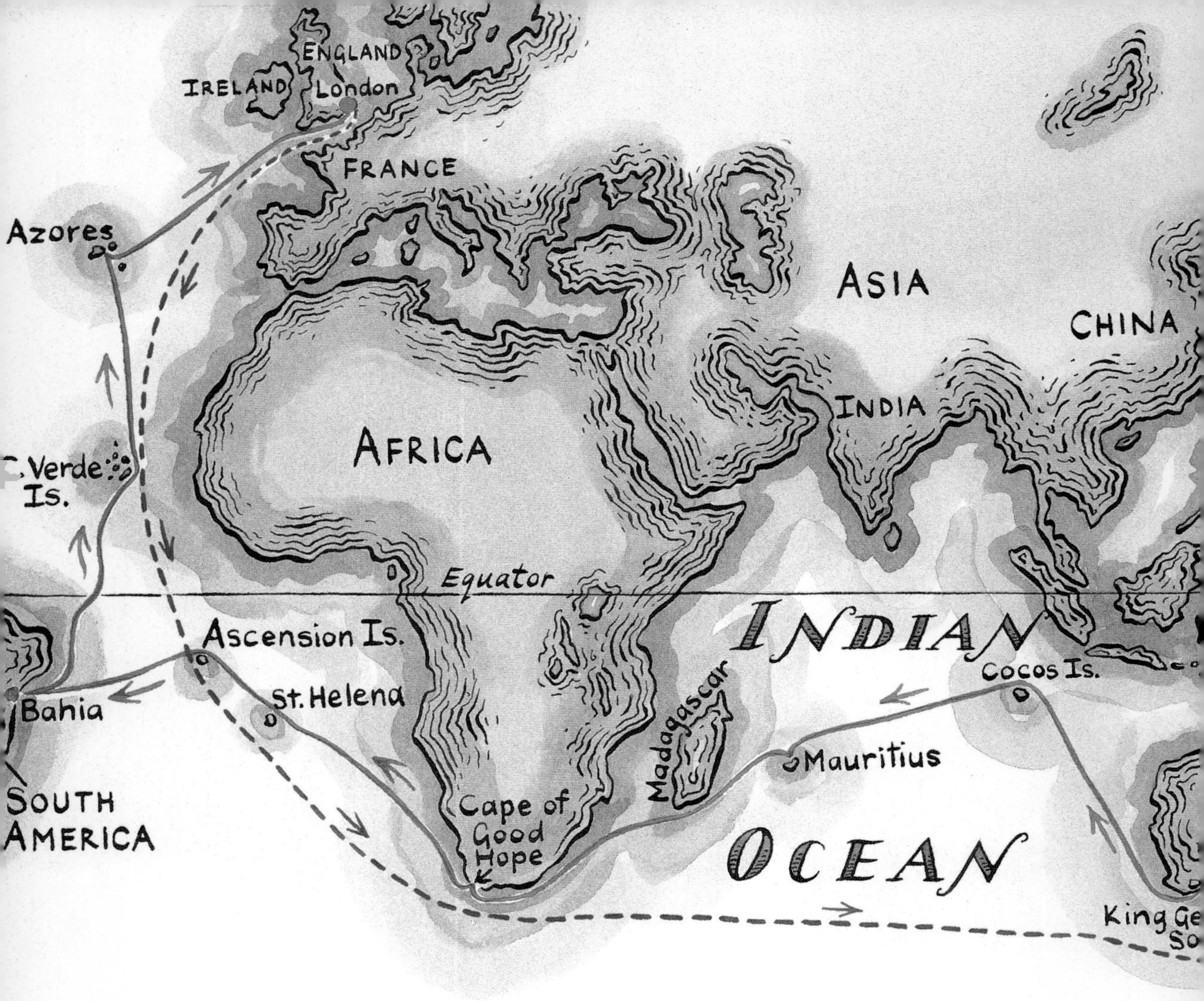
ENGLAND
IRELAND
London
FRANCE
Azores
ASIA
CHINA
INDIA
AFRICA
C. Verde Is.
Equator
INDIAN
Ascension Is.
Cocos Is.
St. Helena
Bahia
Madagascar
Mauritius
SOUTH AMERICA
Cape of Good Hope
OCEAN

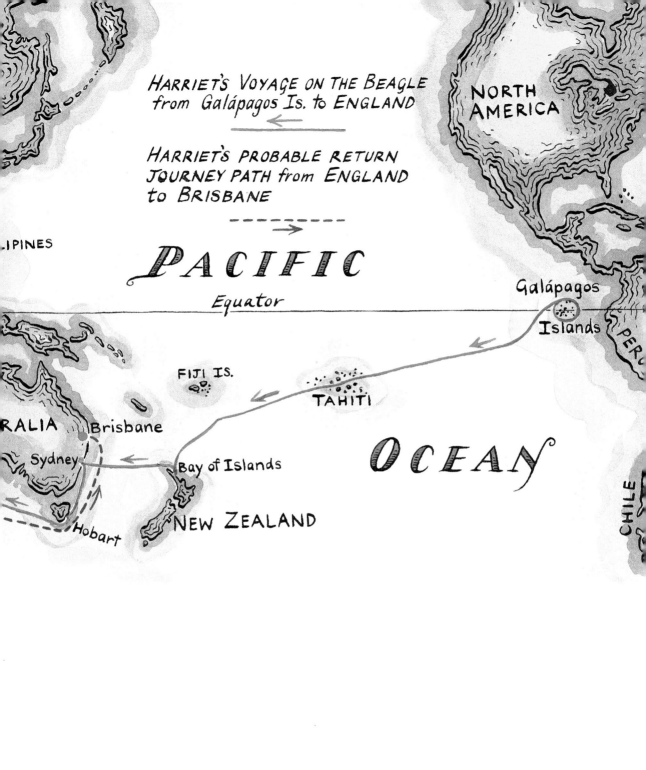

HARRIET'S VOYAGE ON THE BEAGLE
from Galápagos Is. to ENGLAND

HARRIET'S PROBABLE RETURN
JOURNEY PATH from ENGLAND
to BRISBANE

PACIFIC

Equator

NORTH
AMERICA

...IPINES

Galápagos
Islands

PERU

FIJI IS.

TAHITI

OCEAN

...RALIA

Brisbane

Sydney

Bay of Islands

CHILE

Hobart

NEW ZEALAND

Robin Stewart has had a lifelong interest in animals, which she has combined with a career as a teacher and writer.

With her husband Doug, she spent seven years on King Island in Bass Strait, where the couple owned a sheep property and established a penguin-banding and research program on their coastline. Seven years ago they moved to Phillip Island where Robin has been writing full-time, while at the same time studying a nearby muttonbird rookery. Apart from a German shepherd and two Siamese cats, Robin has a stumpy-tailed lizard and breeds blue-tongued lizards. From childhood, Robin has kept pet tortoises, marvelling at their slow, steady progress through time. Animals are a vital part of Robin's life.

For Harriet, my friend

Note: The following story is based largely on documented fact. We can't yet prove Harriet's story; there are shades of truth and proof. It is possible, however, to describe the most likely sequence of events. Gaps have been filled in using the author's imagination.

Prelude

We're standing at the tortoise enclosure at Australia Zoo on Queensland's Sunshine Coast. Famous throughout the world, Australia Zoo is well-known for saltwater crocodiles, dragons, snakes, enormous pythons – and giant tortoises. The zoo loves all animals, but especially those that humans tend to dislike or be afraid of because they aren't warm, cute and cuddly such as koalas, kangaroos and wombats.

The crowd of visitors waits for something to happen. The Galápagos giant tortoise doesn't move a muscle. That's why most of us look into her enclosure and think it's empty. But just as we are beginning to wonder where the tortoise is, one of the large khaki-coloured boulders rises up on four stumpy elephant-like legs and walks slowly to the visitors standing by the low fence. The tortoise's small bright eyes scan the sea of faces, connecting, smiling a greeting to us, her many admirers. Harriet has emerged from stone!

We stare at the huge shell, which is about the size of a medium-sized table, and watch captivated as Harriet moves up and down her sandy pathway. We're waiting for her keeper to arrive, and for the show to begin. Of course, Harriet is the star attraction!

Harriet's enclosure includes a walk-through pool, a rocky cave, boulders and a few trees. They create dark and lighter areas of shade, which allow Harriet to blend into the scenery. Sometimes she is so well-camouflaged that we lose sight of her again. Harriet is playing hide-and-seek with her visitors.

The giant tortoise yawns, her mouth revealing a deep dark hole with a fleshy tongue. Then Harriet stretches out a back leg and lowers herself gently onto the grass. She nibbles some of the fresh green blades, then her eyes wander over to a heap of dry leaves. She's gazing at her bed. Perhaps she is thinking about her mid-afternoon nap.

Like weathered rock, Harriet's legs are covered with an armour of rough scales. Because she can't fold her legs underneath her for protection, these scales keep her safe from predators and stop her body from losing moisture. Harriet's muscles, which she uses for walking and digging, are well-developed. Her feet, which bow out while she walks, support an immense weight. If Harriet were suddenly in danger, she would use her front legs as a shield, to protect her head.

HARRIET'S REPTILE SALAD

By late-morning, the crowd has grown from a dozen or so admirers to a crowd of several hundred. Suddenly, a wildlife keeper appears from behind a solid fence and enters the enclosure. Everyone's eyes move from Harriet to the keeper who is dressed in the typical Australia Zoo uniform – khaki shirt and shorts.

'Welcome to Australia Zoo,' says the young woman. She taps the side of the large, white bucket she is carrying. The bucket is labelled 'Harriet'.

'Harriet always looks forward to her meal-time,' the keeper says. 'And I always look forward to spending time with Harriet, my favourite animal in the world.

'But before I feed Harriet, I want to tell you about her link to one of the most famous scientists of all time,' says the keeper, talking into her microphone. 'It was Charles Darwin who began this story. In 1835, Darwin visited the Galápagos Islands. He discovered Harriet and took her aboard a sailing ship called the *Beagle*, and brought her home with him to

England. Can you believe that all this happened 170 years ago and Harriet is still with us today? Amazing, isn't it?'

Standing tall with her neck outstretched, Harriet moves with slow steady steps towards her smiling keeper and the bucket of food. Tanned and wrinkled by the sun, she sniffs expectantly, while the large crowd murmurs encouraging words to help her along. For an animal carrying such a heavy load, moving anywhere seems a difficult task.

'Every morning Harriet enjoys a special reptile salad that includes string beans, squash, zucchini, eggplant, tomato, mixed lettuce leaves, carrot and parsley. It's a beautifully fresh, balanced and crunchy meal,' says the keeper. 'It even comes with a treat on top. Pink hibiscus flowers. But I'll keep them aside for now.'

After pouring Harriet's meal onto some clean grass, the keeper kneels down beside her and continues, 'Harriet doesn't need teeth. Her jaws are lined with hard sharp edges that cut very efficiently. She could easily snip off one of my fingers, but of course she wouldn't!'

Holding up the three hibiscus flowers, the keeper smiles, 'These are Harriet's favourite food. Her morning treat. They're just like chocolates to us.' Harriet's large, pink, fleshy tongue wraps around the hibiscus flowers and we all click our cameras.

TIME FOR HARRIET'S BATH

Part-way through her meal, Harriet is relaxed enough to enjoy her bath. A teenage boy enters the enclosure, carrying a bucket of warm, soapy water and a kitchen brush. He is a volunteer, and he's being trained to take care of Harriet. He hopes to be Harriet's keeper one day. Everyone wants to be Harriet's keeper!

'Harriet loves her all-over scrub,' says the keeper. 'Can anyone tell me why she needs to have a bath every single day?'

'Because birds sit on her back and do big sloppy poos!' a freckle-faced boy exclaims.

'Yes, you're right! Birds use her as a safe perch. Now, can anyone tell me what other animal does its droppings on Harriet's back?'

'Is it lizards?' answers a young teenage girl.

'Correct again,' says the keeper. 'Hundreds of lizards live free at Australia Zoo. The smartest of them sunbake on Harriet's back. They've learned that Harriet is much better than an ordinary rock. After all, there aren't many rocks that move around to catch the sun's warmth. Harriet is a living solar panel!

'You can see that Harriet's so relaxed about her bath,' continues the keeper, 'that she's started eating again.'

Harriet enjoys having all the lizard and bird droppings washed off her shell. Lovingly, the keeper and volunteer scrub clean every part of her huge dome.

Harriet feels the warm, soapy water and the brush on her shell just as we feel touch to our finger and toe nails. Now that dust, lizard poo and bird droppings are washed off, Harriet's shell is completely clean. It dries quickly in the hot Queensland sun.

Refreshed from her bath, and with her black eyes sparkling, Harriet sighs one of her famous sighs. She loves people. And as her eyes move from face to face, you can tell that she is enjoying our attention.

BEFORE THE DAYS OF ELECTRIC LIGHT, TELEVISION AND THE INTERNET

'This year,' says the keeper, 'Harriet will celebrate her 175th birthday. Can you imagine what it would be like to have lived through the Irish Potato Famine, the Californian and Australian Gold Rushes, through World War I and World War II, and the development of the atomic bomb. Witnessing man's first steps on the moon?

'Try, for a moment, to picture yourself living before the invention of radio, telephones, electric light, aeroplanes, television, cars, satellites, computers, the internet and mobile phones. Before technology such as CDs and PlayStations were even thought of.'

We let our minds wander, imagining the things Harriet must have seen and the changes she would've experienced. Bold and unafraid, Harriet has moved steadily through the years. She is a true survivor.

'Only Harriet, though, can be certain about the exact details of her history,' says the keeper. 'It's her secret. If only we could understand giant tortoise language! If only we could see what those eyes have seen. If only we knew what went on inside that head, behind those small bright eyes. Maybe then we'd be as wise as Harriet.'

IT'S TIME FOR A MASSAGE

The keeper's face and voice soften as she strokes the length of Harriet's shell, then she goes on, 'Harriet's unusually affectionate for a reptile. If you listen carefully you can almost hear her purring! Unfortunately we can't let everyone stroke her. Too much patting by too many different people would tire her out and cause her stress. She's too precious to run that risk. We do have a team of trained volunteers, though, and they are lucky enough to give Harriet plenty of tender loving care.'

Another volunteer enters the giant tortoise enclosure. We watch as she begins to gently stroke Harriet's shell, all of us wishing we could join in. Harriet stops chewing. With a half-eaten lettuce leaf still in her mouth, she rises up on her legs and, standing tall and rigid, slides into a dream-like state.

By standing tall, Harriet's handlers can reach more of her body, especially underneath her shell and 'arm' pits, her deeply wrinkled neck and chin.

'Harriet can remain in this blissful, trance-like state for a very long time,' says the keeper softly, 'for as long as we keep up the massaging. She's one of the gentlest, most loving animals at Australia Zoo.'

The happy holiday crowd grows quiet. It's as if Harriet holds an immense store of energy and calm that she sends out in all directions.

Perhaps Harriet is dreaming…

Dreaming of a beginning, long, long ago.

Dreaming of a faraway island.

Dreaming of eggs buried in sun-warmed sand…

CHAPTER 1
Darwin in the Galápagos

A huge pale moon lights up James Island, one of the many small land masses that make up the Galápagos Islands, which lie off the coast of South America in the Pacific Ocean. The Galápagos Island group was formed by underwater volcanoes, which still erupt today.

Down on the plain, a clutch of giant tortoise eggs begins to quiver and shake with new life. Each egg, nestled in a bed of warm moist sand, has incubated for a period of about six months.

Within the tight confines of his shell, a tortoise hatchling wriggles his toes and flexes his neck. He feels ready to burst! The year is 1830.

The young tortoise chips his way out of the tennis ball-sized egg and through the hard sandy covering. He's been lucky that feral pigs have not uprooted his mother's nest and eaten all the eggs, or that visiting sailors haven't cooked him for breakfast. The tiny hatchling has so far survived.

YOU DON'T MAKE PROGRESS UNLESS YOU STICK YOUR HEAD OUT

Glistening with moisture, the hatchling scampers towards the protection of a prickly shrub on the other side of the clearing. He keeps an eye out for feral cats who would love nothing more than to eat him for dinner. This island is a dangerous place!

A couple of days later, the tortoise hatchling is too busy nibbling on some tender shoots to notice a black rat's beady eyes locked onto him. The rat's whiskers tremble in anticipation of an easy and delicious meal.

Crouching low, the rat concentrates all its muscle-power into its toes, then launches itself at the tortoise.

The tortoise hears a whirr of wings overhead and a Galápagos hawk, on the lookout for a meal, plummets from the sky and grabs the rat in its powerful talons. The rat squeals and kicks wildly to free itself from the needle-sharp claws. But it doesn't escape. The rat is about to become a feast for the hawk!

The hawk flies up to a nearby branch and begins to rip apart its meal. The young tortoise feels his heart might burst through his shell, so hard is it pounding. He has been saved from the rat but will the hawk swoop down and grab him next? In those split seconds, the tortoise thinks he's dead. He feels sure that he'll become dessert for the hawk. But the hawk's belly is full, and a minute or so later, the handsome bird flaps its wings then disappears from the tortoise's view.

Trembling with fear, the tiny tortoise scampers quickly towards a cactus tree, then hides beneath one of its spiky pads. Once again, death has come dangerously close. Until his shell hardens, the tiny hatchling will face danger 24 hours a day.

The young tortoise learns quickly that life in the Galápagos Islands is all about eating, drinking and staying out of reach of birds of prey and feral animals.

Having outlived the dinosaurs and survived all the dangers that 200 million years can throw at a species, the young tortoise adapts to life on James Island. Adaptation is the key to survival.

The tortoise hatchling eats the fleshy cactus pads, soft grasses, flowers and the ripening fruits that grow on this remote, tropical island. Walking to and from a spring-fed pool keeps him well exercised.

By the time the young tortoise is five years old, he is the size of a dinner plate and has grown a hard, horny shell that encloses and protects his body. Life on the island is not as dangerous now. He doesn't have to worry about rats and hawks anymore. He can feast on lush plants and enjoy the feel of warm sun on his shell.

DARWIN IS NOT A GOOD STUDENT

In another part of the world far, far away, lives a young man named Charles Darwin. Charles is not a good student. His father thinks he is a disgrace to the family. 'You care for nothing but shooting, dogs and rat-catching!' he exclaims crossly.

Yet Charles's scientific friends at university are impressed by his love of natural science and his skill in observing, collecting and identifying rare species of plants, birds, insects and other creatures – but especially beetles and the barnacles growing by the seashore.

When Charles Darwin is 23 years old, he's invited to join *HMS Beagle* as companion to Captain FitzRoy. Along with the invitation to be the captain's companion, Charles is offered the position of naturalist. Charles cannot resist the promise of an adventure on board the *Beagle* while also having the chance to study nature.

Back home in Shrewsbury, Charles packs his bags, cramming in trousers, shirts, walking shoes, slippers, a small microscope and telescope, a compass and magnifying glass, nets, notebooks, an atlas and many natural history books. With his bags ready he says goodbye to his family. Part of him feels sad to be leaving home for such a long time. On the other hand, he cannot wait to sail away on the voyage of a lifetime. He hugs his sisters, and his father shakes his hand and wishes him good luck. As he steps into the horse-drawn coach, bound for the seaside port of Plymouth, his brother calls out, "Look after yourself Charles!"

HMS BEAGLE ARRIVES AT THE GALÁPAGOS ISLANDS

The *Beagle*, a small Admiralty vessel measuring 30 metres long by eight metres wide, is on a five-year voyage around the world. In particular, Captain FitzRoy and his officers are going to chart the coastlines of South America. They sail slowly, measuring the depth of the ocean, and making accurate charts and maps. This is the first time the South American coastline has been mapped in detail. Charles is thrilled to be taking part in such an important voyage.

Once the South American part of the voyage is complete, Captain FitzRoy steers the *Beagle* towards the Galápagos Islands. During the 35-day visit in the September and October of 1835, the *Beagle* visits many of the islands in the Galápagos group. Sitting right on the equator in the Pacific Ocean, the Galápagos Islands are about to become very famous.

Charles Darwin, his assistant Syms Covington and three other sailors are put ashore at James Island, which is now known as Isla Santiago, for one week, while the *Beagle* sails on to Chatham Island to fill the ship's tanks with fresh water.

The black sand on James Island stores the powerful rays of the sun in the same way that coal stores the heat of a fire. The sand is so hot that the men can't walk comfortably on it, even while wearing thick boots. The explorers have very little equipment; simply a tent, their bedding and some food. But after all this time at sea, they are used to roughing it.

Running in front of the men and resembling miniature dragons, thousands of marine iguanas slither from the rocks and plunge into the ocean. But it's the burrows of the land iguana that make it difficult for the men to find a place to pitch their tent. There are many cormorants, all with shrivelled wings, penguins and sea lions, giant tortoises feeding on cactus pads, land iguanas climbing cactus trees that are ten metres tall and many species of unique land birds – and every one of them amazingly tame.

Darwin, Covington and their companions believe they've entered another world, a place that looks like the beginning of time. They pitch their tent in a small valley not far from the beach. There is one big problem though: they can't find safe drinking water.

The explorers decide to search for water inland. They walk up into the mountains where lush vegetation grows over the misty peaks.

The walking soon tires them, so Darwin and Covington come up with the idea of hitching a ride. Cautiously, they approach a pair of giant tortoises nibbling on a nearby cactus. Darwin is surprised to find that they don't try to move away, or even hide their heads beneath their massive shells. Darwin lets his fingers trail over one of their hard horny shells. Carefully, the men climb onto the tortoises' backs. They ride them like horses along a well-defined track. Because so many animals seem to use the track, Darwin guesses that it will almost certainly end up at a small pond. And it does exactly that. Thanks to the tortoises, Darwin has discovered an all-important, permanent source of fresh spring water!

THE HAUNT OF PIRATES

James Island is a favourite haunt of pirates, with Buccaneer Bay their special landing place. With lots of secret bays to hide in, plenty of whaling ships to attack and rob, fresh drinking water and tortoise meat, it's easy to see why James Island is so popular. The pirates kill and eat hundreds of giant tortoises. They also collect dazzling white salt of the finest quality from a crater lake on the island. They use it to preserve tortoise meat, as well as to improve the flavour of their other foods. The pirates think of the giant tortoises as 'living lunchboxes'.

Having survived feral animals and birds of prey, will the young tortoise end up as food for pirates?

DARWIN'S DINNER PLATES

Using his sharp, horny mouth as a knife, the young tortoise snips off a juicy piece of cactus. Chewing rhythmically, with eyes half-closed, he hasn't noticed the approach of a man.

When Darwin scoops him up, the tortoise opens his small bright eyes in astonishment. Nothing in his five years of life has prepared him for this. Yet he doesn't struggle or attempt to bite those hands. Rather, he squirms uncomfortably, pulls in his wrinkly neck to protect his head – then does a very large, sloppy poo. Right down Darwin's leg.

But Darwin doesn't mind. He is far too busy looking into the young tortoise's curious eyes.

Still young and only the size of a dinner plate, Darwin can examine the tortoise easily. Everything about giant tortoises fascinates Darwin. Their hard, horny dome-shaped shells are layered with tough, dry plates of skin. Their stumpy legs are covered with small, horny scales while each foot is equipped with five short, blunt claws.

Never before has Darwin considered taking live animals back to London. All his other specimens are preserved and very much dead. But he is so intrigued by giant tortoises that he has already placed two in a box to take with him on the voyage home.

'This will be the third and last tortoise to take back with us to London,' Darwin calls out to Covington.

Covington reaches out his hands to take the young tortoise,

and Darwin continues, 'When we get back on board the *Beagle* this afternoon, you can put him in the box with the other two.'

'He looks just a little bit different from the others,' comments Covington, as he slips the tortoise into the cloth bag that hangs over his shoulder. Darwin agrees, and wonders why this is so.

Covington spends their last few hours on James Island collecting a sack full of tortoise food: berries, cactus pads, feathery leaves and lush grasses, many of which grow in the misty mountains. Enough to feed three tortoises for the next few weeks.

When the young tortoise finds himself enclosed in the bag, he does what most animals would do in this circumstance. He plays dead. Keeping perfectly still usually confuses an attacker, who will then lose interest and wander away. So the young tortoise thinks, 'If I act as if I'm no longer alive perhaps this horrible event will pass, with no more danger?'

So he shuts his eyes tightly and slips into a type of sleep. A sleep that lasts until Covington, still carrying the cloth bag over his shoulder, climbs aboard the *Beagle*.

After their week on James Island, Captain FitzRoy welcomes Darwin and his crew back on board. It's time to set sail again for distant lands.

BACK ON THE *BEAGLE*

The small sailing ship rises and falls in an easy swell, her sails fluttering in the gentle breeze. Darwin and Covington watch as James Island disappears from view. The date is 20 October 1835.

In his role as the *Beagle*'s naturalist, Darwin, with Covington's help, has collected 38 different types of plant life that grow in the Galápagos Islands. Thirty of these can only be found on James Island. On land or sea, Darwin and Covington are always busy. As well as Galápagos Island plant specimens, they've collected rocks, eggs, insects, seashells, and bird and reptile skins. Most of the plants and creatures are unique to the Galápagos Islands; they are found nowhere else in the world.

Darwin's small cabin contains a remarkable collection. Every space is full, yet the *Beagle* faces a 12-month voyage back to England, a journey that will take them three-quarters of the way around the globe.

SHIPWRECKS AND TORTOISE BOXES

On the deck, Darwin bends over to examine the two tortoise boxes that Covington has assembled. They've been built from driftwood, collected from shipwrecks. One box contains two young tortoises, the other stores their food. Dry barnacles cling to the silvery wood, along with strands of seaweed bleached by the tropical sun.

'You've done a good job,' says Darwin to Covington. 'There's plenty of room for three tortoises. But I think we need another length of rope to tie the boxes more securely.'

NAMING THE TRIO

Although the young tortoises are from different Galápagos islands, and are therefore different types of tortoises, at this age they look similar. There are, however, slight variations when Darwin and Covington examine them carefully.

'Let's call them Tom, Dick and Harry,' suggests Covington, his eyes twinkling with amusement.

'They're good nicknames,' agrees Darwin, 'especially since we don't know whether they're male or female. But look, Harry's shell is a little darker than his mates'. And whereas Tom's shell is slightly smaller, Dick's legs look a bit longer.

'Tom, Dick and Harry,' murmurs Darwin, with a smile, 'quite a trio. Tom from Chatham Island; that's where Captain FitzRoy filled the *Beagle*'s water tanks. Remember that fresh water cascading down the cliffs, and all those volcanic cones?'

'And Dick, from Charles Island,' continues Covington, 'where it took ten men to lift that one tortoise onto the whaling ship.

'And you'll be Harry. Harry from James Island,' Covington whispers to the young tortoise as he lowers him into the driftwood box.

Harry hisses. He hates being confined to a box. He doesn't like the other tortoises. He isn't amused at all by those two faces peering down at him. So he decides to hide and tucks his head beneath his shell. Now he feels safe. Then he shuts his eyes tight, imagining lots of space. He thinks of sunshine warming his shell.

Darwin runs his fingers lightly over Harry's domed shell, feeling the pattern. 'How perfectly formed,' he says to Covington. 'Soft yet hard. Light yet dark. Neither wet nor entirely dry. A living wonder as ancient as prehistoric forests.'

Noticing how anxious Harry has become, Covington says, 'He'll settle down, but it'll take a few days.'

But Harry isn't sure about that. Where are his cactus trees? Why can't he get out of the box? The ground beneath his feet has disappeared. The sky hangs low. His whole world seems upside down! All he can see are strange, staring faces, coils of rope, one of the three masts and beyond, only gulls.

More frightening, though, is the rocking sensation as the ship moves up and down in the swell. It makes Harry feel sick in the stomach, and unbalanced. As if he needs to hang onto something.

SAILING TO TAHITI

Leaving behind the Galápagos Islands, the *Beagle* sets sail for Tahiti. Tom, Dick and Harry hear the slap and splash of water against the timber hull, and see a light wind fill the sails as the *Beagle* heads in a south-westerly direction across the Pacific Ocean.

All 72 men on board are pleased to be heading for home. For four years, occasional letters from England have been their only link with family and friends, and there have been long periods of time without any mail at all. Darwin and Covington spend a lot of time in Darwin's cabin, using Darwin's microscope and dissecting tools to examine sea creatures. They record their observations in a notebook.

Regularly, they visit Harry and his companions. Darwin and Covington spend many hours discussing the tortoise trio and wondering about the slight differences between them. Do these differences mean anything?

Fortunately, the three young tortoises don't know that 13 fully grown tortoises are on board as well. These giants are turned over on their backs and lie helpless on the after-deck, ready to be killed and eaten during the long voyage home.

'There's nothing so deliciously sweet to eat,' say the sailors, 'than roast tortoise meat.' The usual diet of salted meat, pickled vegetables and biscuits gets very tiresome, especially on a long ocean voyage.

It never occurs to Harry that, in the event of a food shortage, he may end up as tortoise soup for hungry sailors. It certainly is a very real possibility though, for in the 1800s, eating giant tortoises and riding on their backs was considered neither cruel nor damaging to the environment. Back then, most people didn't worry about endangered species. Nor did they feel concern when an animal became extinct. After all, according to the Bible, God created animals for humans to use.

LIVING ABOARD *HMS BEAGLE*

Every day Covington checks Harry and his two companions, scoops droppings out of their box, then tosses the waste overboard. Fresh cactus pads, as well as lush grasses, mosses and ferns are offered to the tortoises. They also get fresh drinking water but the trio seem thirsty only every second or third day – and can last up to one week without wanting any water at all.

While he cares for them, Covington talks to the tortoises, and soon Harry becomes accustomed to Covington's cheerful chatter and the merry sound of his fiddle. And as the *Beagle* rides the ocean swell, and the decks heave, Harry learns to recognise Covington and Darwin by their faces, voices and the feel of their hands. Little by little, he feels more at ease with his human carers.

Gradually, the days of clear blue skies and billowing sails become less strange to the trio of tortoises confined to their box.

SEASICK TORTOISES

One morning, when the *Beagle* is mid-Pacific Ocean, Harry senses a change in the air. His nostrils twitch. Far away he detects the rumble of thunder. Tom and Dick don't notice the change. Nor does Captain FitzRoy. It is many hours later before any of the sailors recognise the signs of bad weather approaching.

The storm hits the *Beagle* with an almighty whack. The small sailing ship rolls about in the swell, tossing like a gull's feather caught in a gale. Darwin's face changes from a healthy pink colour to a greyish-green. When he begins to feel sick in the stomach, Darwin leaves his cabin and goes to sit on the deck, close to the tortoises' box. He vomits frequently over the side of the ship – in spite of all the fresh air.

Through the top of the box, Harry sees sailors scrambling up the rope rigging. Captain FitzRoy is shouting commands. Ropes are tightened. Sails are set.

On another level, and through cracks in the side of the box, Harry watches the legs of sailors. Running legs, moving swiftly through sheets of seawater.

Timber is creaking. Wind moans through the sails.

Tom, Dick and Harry feel sick.

The young tortoises crouch miserably as they're thrown from one side of the box to the other. After a few hours Harry is exhausted. His legs tremble as the wind roars through the rigging. He wonders whether it will ever be calm again. Harry hears Dick sighing softly and sees a look of terror on Tom's face. Will they survive the storm?

Every now and then, waves crash over the deck and salty water splashes onto Darwin and the tortoises. Darwin's clothes become crusty with salt. Harry tastes the salt water and spits it out in disgust. He is *not* a sea turtle.

After what seems a very long time, the storm blows itself out. By the following day the ocean is calm, as if exhausted by the tumultuous weather. Darwin is able to go back to his cabin, to continue work on his collection of specimens. Meanwhile, Tom, Dick and Harry's appetite returns and they eat small quantities of the juicy cactus leaf that Covington offers.

ISLANDS OF PLENTY: A TROPICAL PARADISE

Half way to New Zealand, the *Beagle* arrives at the small volcanic island of Tahiti. This part of the voyage has taken 25 days. As soon as the *Beagle* drops anchor, the ship is surrounded by canoes crowded with excited natives. Against a backdrop of rocky peaks, gently sloping hills and lush tropical vegetation, the laughter and happy voices of men, women and children welcome the captain and crew of the *Beagle*.

Tom, Dick and Harry stay in their box aboard the *Beagle* while Darwin and Covington explore the mountains and a nearby coral reef. Meanwhile, for the 18 days that the *Beagle* stays in Tahitian waters, the crew feasts on lush tropical fruits and vegetables. Some of the sailors share the best of the fruit with the three young giant tortoises. Tom loves the tang of pineapple, Dick prefers breadfruit and Harry adores banana. It's at this stage, though, that Darwin introduces Harry to hibiscus flowers and he loves them with a passion.

Before the *Beagle* leaves Tahiti, Captain FitzRoy invites the Queen of Tahiti to visit his ship. Four boats carry the royal party from the island to the sailing ship. Harry sees some of the flags decorating the ship and hears the Queen, escorted by chiefs, welcomed aboard by Captain FitzRoy.

Once the guests are served tea, Tom, Dick and Harry listen to the entertainment provided by the seamen. Covington's fiddle sets a merry mood as the sailors sing their ditties.

After the singing and story-telling, Tom, Dick and Harry hear the sound of strange voices and many footsteps drawing near. They look up and there looms the large, plump face of the Queen of Tahiti.

'For eating?' she mimes, her gaze on the three young tortoises.

'No,' says Captain FitzRoy, shaking his head. 'Darwin's tortoises are for scientific study.' The Queen looks confused, so the captain pretends to be Darwin writing in his notebook. Still the Queen appears puzzled. To her, plants and animals are for eating.

From these 'islands of plenty', Covington fills the tortoises' food box with bananas, coconuts, breadfruit, bamboo shoots, banana leaves and large glossy breadfruit leaves. Plenty to last the three and a half weeks until they reach their next destination. On 3 December 1835, at first light, the *Beagle* pulls anchor and sets sail for New Zealand.

STOP-OVER IN NEW ZEALAND

With the wind in her sails, the *Beagle* approaches the northern-most tip of New Zealand. They drop anchor at the Bay of Islands. Once ashore, Darwin and Captain FitzRoy walk around the village, talking to the Maori men, women and children. Darwin is astounded by the black tattoos that decorate their faces. Darwin and the captain are taught the local custom of pressing noses as a form of greeting and respect.

Meanwhile Covington sets to work replenishing the tortoises' food box. From an English cottage garden, he collects handfuls of clover, fresh green grass, rose leaves and petals, honeysuckle and sweet-briar. Enough to feed the tortoises for the next two weeks.

'Tom and Dick seem to like clover best,' says Darwin, watching as the two giant tortoises take great mouthfuls of the fresh green leaves.

'Yet Harry prefers rose petals,' observes Covington, 'especially the red ones. Perhaps they taste like hibiscus flowers.'

MOONSTRUCK

Along a silvery pathway connecting Earth to the moon, fly thousands of slim, dark seabirds. Looking upwards out of the driftwood box, Harry watches as the petrels flap, float and glide, flying close together, using the moon and stars to find their way.

Harry stretches his neck to get a better view, and then relaxes into the box again. Tom and Dick are sound asleep. Harry yawns widely then slips into a peaceful dream.

AUSTRALIA THEN HEADING FOR LONDON

The *Beagle*'s first Australian stop-over is Port Jackson, a mooring close to the town of Sydney. It is January 1836. Darwin hires a guide and two horses to take him up into the Blue Mountains. On one of his rest breaks, besides Cox's River, Darwin sees platypuses diving and playing in a chain of pools. These mysterious creatures have a bill like a duck, webbed feet like a frog, venom like a snake, fur like a seal, nest and eggs like a bird, and a tail like a beaver. Darwin has never seen anything like them. And never will again.

But the eucalypt forests, stretching out in all directions, do not impress Darwin and Covington. The trees look untidy, with peculiar pale green leaves. It's difficult to imagine anything eating the leaves, let alone giant tortoises who relish the tropical fruits of Tahiti.

'Gum leaves are much too leathery to use for tortoise food,' says Darwin.

'I agree,' replies Covington, as he picks a few leaves then crushes them between his fingers. 'Have a smell of these,' he continues, handing over the crushed fragments to Darwin.

'A very strong and peculiar aroma,' agrees Darwin. 'Oily too. We'll have to find other food.'

But there isn't much else in the Sydney area. Certainly nothing tropical or succulent, so dry grasses and feathery acacia leaves fill the box. When Covington offers the tortoises some of the dry grass and acacia leaves, they turn their heads away. After a few minutes, though, Harry's eyes lock onto some golden balls of wattle blossom.

'Yes,' thinks Harry, 'I'll try some of these, but not that other stuff.'

Hobart, on the other hand, offers lush grass and rose petals, as well as lettuce, beans and corn cobs. But no bananas or hibiscus flowers. In Western Australia, coarse wiry grass and acacia leaves are tossed into the tortoises' box. By this stage, however, Harry is not as fussy. Resignedly he munches his way through acacia leaves and even eats a few mouthfuls of grass.

The islands in the Indian Ocean produce different types of food. Each stop-over has its own bank of fluffy, white cloud and its own seabirds. On the Cocos Islands, gulls hover just clear of the one mast Harry can see, while a warm breeze blows gently through the sails. Soon the *Beagle* is anchored and the men go ashore.

When Darwin and Covington return to the ship they come laden with fresh tasty pumpkin, coconut palm leaves and sweet fruits, which they stuff into the food box. The giant tortoises eat with enthusiasm. There are even bananas for Harry!

The Indian Ocean island of Mauritius offers Darwin a ride on the back of the island's only elephant, while further south-west, the *Beagle* crew catch sight of the large island of Madagascar – famous for its monkey-like lemurs.

After rounding the Cape of Good Hope – the southern-most tip of Africa – and stopping briefly at Cape Town, the *Beagle* sails into a fierce gale. But a day later she's becalmed. Without wind, a sailing ship goes nowhere.

Eventually though, a breeze turns into a light wind and the *Beagle* sails once more – slicing through the water like a sharp knife.

The volcanic island of St. Helena in the southern Atlantic Ocean rises from the sea like an enormous castle. The *Beagle* drops anchor and lowers a small boat over the side. After rowing a short distance, the sailors pull into a sheltered cove. Darwin and Covington step ashore. Covington, always on the lookout for tortoise food, comes upon a dense thicket of blackberry vines, laden with fruit. As the men feast on the berries, Covington collects a bundle of blackberry leaves and berries to fill the tortoises' dwindling larder, along with some lush green grass.

Back on board the *Beagle*, Tom and Dick eat the blackberry leaves. Harry, on the other hand, greedily snatches all the blackberries until his mouth turns purple.

On to South America and Bahia where coconuts, bananas, mangoes and oranges grow in abundance. Then to Cape Verde Islands where there is nothing much at all. Here, the volcanic nature of the islands, combined with the hot tropical sun, reduces the tortoises' food box to desert plants. But the tortoises prove they can adapt to anything, anywhere. They have not outlived the dinosaurs to turn up their toes and die on the *Beagle*.

THE MYSTERY OF THE GIANT TORTOISES

Slow-moving, heavily armoured reptiles first appeared on Earth about 200 million years ago. What's amazing though, is that giant tortoises have remained almost unchanged for 150 million years!

As Darwin lies in his narrow hammock bed aboard the *Beagle*, he thinks about the mystery of giant tortoises. Giant tortoises live in their natural state in only two places in the entire world: the Galápagos Islands in the Pacific Ocean, and Aldabra Island in the Indian Ocean. The two types are different; they are not the same species. So why is it that giant tortoises have survived on these two groups of remote islands when they have died out everywhere else?

NEARING HOME

The island of Terceira, in the Azores, is their last stop-over. Darwin visits a volcanic crater and sees jets of steam spurting from cracks in the rock. During his walk, Darwin recognises some English migratory birds and immediately feels a deep longing to be home. It's lucky, then, that his journey is coming to an end.

On the first day of October, in 1836, Harry senses a change of mood aboard the *Beagle*. A certain restlessness as the small sailing ship comes in sight of Land's End, then heads towards the nearby English port of Falmouth. Harry feels the *Beagle* drift slowly towards a mooring. He raises his head and sniffs the cool, moist air.

It's almost one year since Tom, Dick and Harry were captured on the Galápagos Islands. Almost five years since Captain FitzRoy, Darwin, Covington and crew left England to embark on their adventure aboard the *Beagle*.

The voyage is ending, but its effect on the way we view life on Earth is just beginning.

Change is in the air. Big change.

Change can be for better or for worse.

Will the giant tortoises survive the cold, wet climate of England?

CHAPTER 2
Bone-chilling English winters

On a dark and rainy night on Sunday, 2 October 1836, the *Beagle* anchors at the English port of Falmouth. Although the sailing ship has not yet reached its final destination, Darwin leaps ashore and catches the first mail coach to his home town of Shrewsbury.

'It's so good to be back in England!' Darwin exclaims to a fellow traveller. 'To be on dry land again. It's almost five years since I left home and sailed away on the *Beagle*. I can hardly wait to see my family and friends.'

As the horse-drawn coach rushes through the stormy night, Darwin reflects on the excitement of the past five years. 'I've sailed on a voyage into the unknown, I've been bitten by bedbugs, escaped an attack by a puma, and survived earthquakes and a tsunami,' he remembers, as squalls of heavy rain lash the windows of the coach. 'I've suffered seasickness and survived the dangers of horrendous storms at sea. And I've seen with my own eyes the wonders of Nature, especially in the Galápagos Islands.'

After two tiring days on the road, Darwin is relieved to arrive at Shrewsbury and to be welcomed by his family and friends. He has left Tom, Dick and Harry in Covington's care until the *Beagle* reaches its final destination.

FROM THE *BEAGLE* TO A TERRACE HOUSE IN LONDON

Finally the *Beagle* sails up the Thames River and anchors at Greenwich, a borough of Greater London. After spending some time in Shrewsbury, Darwin travels to London where he hires a horse-drawn coach to carry his belongings – which include the three tortoises and his enormous collection of specimens – to his London house at 36 Great Marlborough Street.

Harry is bursting with curiosity to know what's happening, so he peers through the cracks in the box, catching glimpses of people's legs as they rush around. His nostrils flare at the smell of smoke and the black, sooty air. Weak sun falls from a sky that hangs low with dense, grey cloud. The tortoises hear the sound of wheels on fine gravel. Instead of the rocking movement of the *Beagle*, Tom, Dick and Harry feel the steady forward momentum of the coach as it travels the short distance between Greenwich and Darwin's new home. Once in the city, though, the iron-rimmed cartwheels clatter along the cobbled streets and Harry feels as though all the bones in his body are rattling around like loose stones.

The three tortoises are not afraid. But they are curious, so they listen attentively as horses whinny and men shout until the coach reaches its destination. Darwin and Covington help to unload countless boxes and crates of specimens into the tall terrace house.

Finally, the box containing the three Galápagos giant tortoises is carried indoors. The tortoises are the only live creatures to have been collected. All the rest are dead. Snakes, spiders, beetles, birds, small mammals and iguanas, all arranged in neat piles in a cold, draughty room with spider webs hanging from the tall ceiling.

After spending almost 12 months at sea, the three tortoises are used to the continual rolling motion of a ship and find it difficult to adjust to life on land. For seven days or so, Harry feels quite wobbly until he gets his land legs again.

Within a day, Covington cleans away the spider webs and

constructs a roomy indoor tortoise enclosure that is lit up with occasional rays of sunshine. Several piles of dry oak leaves provide hiding places where the trio can sleep undisturbed. Covington removes their droppings every day, changes the water in their drinking bowl and feeds them grass, lettuce leaves, string beans, carrots and dandelion leaves. But unfortunately for Harry, there are no bananas or hibiscus flowers – his favourite things.

After his meal, Harry feels gentle hands lifting him from the enclosure. He becomes aware of someone examining his shell. Harry sees weak sunlight and shadows filtering indoors through the leaves and branches of a tree growing outside in the tiny garden. Harry's greatest strength is his ability to adapt to any environment, no matter how strange. So, although he remembers living free in the Galápagos Islands, Harry doesn't mind being indoors in London.

WINTER APPROACHES

The tortoises are beginning to notice the climate. It's cold. Winter is fast approaching and, when compared to the hot, steamy, tropical conditions of the Galápagos Islands, the climate change comes as a shock to the young giant tortoises.

Every few days an icy wind blows in from the north-east and slaps at the windows above the tortoise enclosure. Within only one month of arriving in England, the tortoises are getting their first taste of an English winter. Harry remembers feeling hot sunshine on his shell. He thinks of sun-warmed volcanic rock and marine iguanas slithering into the sea. This cold, gloomy weather is not to his liking, not at all.

As well as noticing the cold, Harry observes all the comings and goings of Darwin's busy household. He watches Darwin and Covington go about their daily business. His nose twitches with the warm, yeasty smells coming from the kitchen, while at night he listens to the yowls and screams of fighting street cats – along with the high-pitched squeaks of mice scampering about in the ceiling.

Darwin receives a lot of letters, from scientist friends all over the world. Every morning Harry watches while Darwin carefully breaks open the sealing wax of each envelope, takes out the letter then reads it. Harry also recognises the sounds of Covington's pen as he copies thousands of names onto paper using his best copperplate writing. Sometimes Covington uses steel pen-nibs. At other times though, he and Darwin use goose-feather quills dipped in ink.

While Covington is busy recording information, Darwin is studying and classifying the thousands of specimens he collected during the five-year *Beagle* voyage and, together with his detailed notes, begins the task of solving the mystery of how life began on Earth. It will take years of patient research and investigation before his daring theory is announced to the world.

A TORTOISE FOR EACH ISLAND

When Darwin was in the Galápagos Islands, Vice Governor Lawson, the acting governor of the Galápagos Islands, mentioned that he was able to tell which island a giant tortoise came from by simply looking at the shape of its shell. This conversation keeps coming back to Darwin over and over again while he studies the specimens he brought back with him. It seems like a clue, a clue that will continue to prod Darwin until he solves the biggest riddle of all time: the origins of life on Earth.

'Why are there differences between the tortoises,' Darwin wonders, 'when the islands are so close together? Has God created a different type of tortoise for each Galápagos island, each one perfectly suited to its surroundings? But what if something else has happened? Something that no one has thought of before?'

In early 1837, Darwin takes the three young tortoises to the British Museum, to be examined by the reptile expert John Gray. Darwin hopes that variations will be found that will identify the tortoises as different types.

After picking up and examining each tortoise in turn, John Gray says, 'I'm sorry Mr Darwin, but they're too immature to compare with one another. They need to be older before I can scientifically measure their differences. Ideally they need to be 30 to 40 years of age. But I must warn you, though. No giant tortoise has survived in this climate for more than a couple of years. The cold is like a death sentence.'

Darwin is disappointed. He knows the three young tortoises come from different islands in the Galápagos group. He believes mature giant tortoises vary from island to island. But he will have to be patient and wait until they mature. If they mature.

THE BIG CHILL

At first the tortoises don't feel more than a slight discomfort in the cold, but as January progresses, Harry feels a chill creeping into his bones. He shivers, then pulls his head in under his shell. 'It's warmer this way,' he thinks, 'tucked up beneath my shell. I'll stay here until it turns warm again.'

In a room of his own in the attic, Covington feels cold as well. He has only a small lamp, a stool, a bed and his few possessions. But the light of the lamp is dim, and the windows are wet with a dirty fog. Long, long winter nights. Time to dream. Often Covington wishes he were back sailing on the *Beagle*, in the warmth of the tropics.

In spite of Covington's excellent care, the giant tortoises become more and more lethargic. He tries to tempt their appetites with small sticks of crunchy carrot, freshly shelled green peas, strawberries and edible mushrooms. But they hardly eat anything, only a few raw mushrooms. As a result, Covington rarely has to clean up their droppings.

By February, Tom, Dick and Harry's level of activity has slowed right down, along with their breathing, pulse rate and appetite. Their skin becomes cold to the touch. They don't respond to handling. Their eyes are closed. Covington remarks that they look almost dead. They have, in fact, slipped into a slowing-down, sleep-like condition known as hibernation – a protective response against the freezing winter temperatures of London.

In the Galápagos Islands, intolerable heat triggers a similar response. But in the Galápagos Islands, the giant tortoises can soak in the cool water of a spring, or dig a hole in moist, cool sand.

SLIDING INTO A STATE OF NUMBNESS

Tom, Dick and Harry feel numb from their toes upwards. A chill seeps through their blunt claws and into their stumpy elephant-like legs. The creeping coldness spreads into their internal organs and the horny armour of their shell.

Harry feels himself closing up like a tight fist, with his shell protecting his body. 'Is this what dying feels like?' he wonders. 'Or is this terrible cold something else?' Harry is the first to burrow into the thick layer of slightly moist sand lining the floor of their indoor enclosure. Tom and Dick follow a few days later. Darwin takes note of the dates on the calendar while Covington spreads a mixture of hay and pieces of loose bark over the hibernating tortoises.

A cold mist hangs heavy over London. Covington stokes the fire in the grate with a few chunks of coal, then wipes the fogged up windowpane with the sleeve of his shirt. All he can

see are bare trees. A draught circles the room, while outside, ice holds the grass stiff, and the ground begins to freeze.

A cold north wind rattles the windows as Darwin bends over the tortoise enclosure, his eyebrows knitted with worry and anxiety. He turns to Covington saying, 'I've been told that they could suffer a serious illness such as rheumatism or pneumonia while experiencing their first-ever hibernation. And that they could die.'

Blowing on his hands to warm them, Covington replies, 'It isn't even mid-winter. It'll only get worse.'

'Another worry,' says Darwin, 'is the smoky, polluted air we're all breathing. It's unhealthy and damages our lungs. Even the garden plants and trees are suffering. You only have to touch the foliage and your fingers are smeared with soot and grime.'

WAKING FROM A DEEP SLEEP

By mid-April 1837, Covington hears rustling sounds coming from the tortoise enclosure. They are starting to stir! Harry's first signs of life are very slow and careful. He wakes up gradually. It's like emerging from a dream, when you drift in and out of sleep many times before waking properly. Harry feels his skin prickling as if thousands of tiny pins are piercing his body. The sensation makes him restless. Only his shell remains unaffected.

Harry wriggles his toes, stretches out a back leg then opens his eyes a little. He blinks a few times, his eyes absorbing the gentle light of spring. Then he opens his eyes fully and sees Darwin and Covington. Rising up on his legs, Harry stands then takes a few wobbly steps towards the men.

'Thank God he didn't die,' says Covington, as he lifts Harry up and carries the tortoise from his enclosure indoors to a tiny outside garden area.

Within hours, Tom and Dick also wake from their hibernation. Darwin carries Dick to the outside enclosure, his fingers clasped firmly on either side of the tortoise's shell. Covington follows with Tom.

'I've been worried all through this long, cold winter,' Darwin admits as he lowers Dick onto the grass. 'I'd hate to think of them dying because I took them from the tropical climate of the Galápagos Islands to the cold of London. I didn't realise their first hibernation was such a risk. Sometimes I wish we hadn't taken them at all. It's such a relief to see them awake again.'

Within the tiny garden, Covington has built an enclosure,

which includes a shallow pool. Warm spring sunshine floods the area and it isn't long before all three giant tortoises are taking experimental bites of the shrubbery, fresh green grasses and spring flowers.

'It was a good idea,' says Darwin to Covington, 'to wash the soot off the grass and garden plants. I am sure it's made the greenery taste a lot better.'

After waking from his deep sleep, Harry is ravenous. He smells garden flowers in the warm air. He hears a thrush singing nearby, and sees a leafless tree bursting with buds. He tastes the spring grasses, but especially loves the sweetness of clover. Stretching his neck, he snips off some new buds then chews them thoughtfully. He sniffs the freshness of spring and feels warmth soaking into his shell.

During the cooler summer days, the giant tortoises are moved back indoors where they are kept in a sunroom enclosure. A summer's day in London is never as warm as a summer's day in the Galápagos Islands!

After a week or so, Darwin says to Covington, 'Have a look at their shells. They're covered with tiny specks of soot. I think it'd be a good idea to give them a bath.'

Covington fetches a bucket of warm, soapy water and a

kitchen sponge. Harry feels the warm water on his shell. But when Covington gently washes his wrinkly neck, Harry stretches out his neck for more. He loves the feeling of the water. This is his very first bath!

The bath is so refreshing that Harry suddenly feels more active and listens more attentively to the rattling of cabs and coaches as they travel along the nearby cobbled street.

'Now that I've washed them, you can see the colour of their shells,' remarks Covington.

'And the patterns are a little different on each. And they're all shades of brown and khaki,' observes Darwin. 'The plates are quite attractive now that they're clean.'

QUESTIONS AND MORE QUESTIONS

Although the tortoises cannot, at this age, be identified as different types, Darwin and Covington can tell them apart. Tom is, and always has been, slightly smaller than Harry and Dick. And Dick has longer legs, with one pale-coloured front claw. To Darwin, these slight differences seem to be of immense importance. He can't stop thinking about them.

'If God created Heaven and Earth, as well as all living

things, in just six days,' wonders Darwin, 'why did he allow certain animals to become extinct?'

Thinking back to his experiences in South America, Darwin remembers finding the fossilised remains of a giant armadillo, and the remains of a rodent the size of a rhinoceros. And huge fossilised oyster shells – animals that are now extinct.

'But why do these fossilised remains resemble the smaller-sized animals of today? Life was meant to be the same now as on the day of creation – but it's not!' thinks Darwin.

'Why did the dinosaurs die out when similar reptiles such as crocodiles, lizards and tortoises did not? Was it simply a matter of good luck? Or God's will?

'Giant tortoises must be one of Nature's most successful designs,' thinks Darwin, as he gazes thoughtfully at Tom, Dick and Harry. Darwin examines their shells. Each is coloured in a way that helps them blend into the earth, sand, rock and vegetation of their environment.

Darwin thinks back to the Galápagos Islands, to that mysterious landscape of volcanoes and black lava, cactus trees and giant tortoises. 'Why have giant tortoises survived on the Galápagos Islands and Aldabra Island (in the Indian Ocean) when in all other parts of the world they have died out?

Everywhere else in the world, tortoises have become smaller and smaller in size.

'Is it because they live in extreme isolation,' Darwin wonders, 'quite separate from the continents of South America and Africa? Is this the reason why Galápagos animals and plants are so different to everything else on Earth? But why do they also vary from island to island, when the islands are within sight of each other! What's going on?' Darwin asks himself.

As Darwin bends over his microscope, peering closely at the feathery feelers of a barnacle, he asks Covington, 'How do you think that Galápagos tortoises benefit from being so huge?'

'Maybe it helps them survive,' replies Covington, 'in times of drought.'

'Yes,' agrees Darwin. 'They're certainly able to store massive quantities of fat and water. So much so, they can survive on ships with no food or water for 12 months.'

Patiently they continue sorting out, examining and recording Darwin's Galápagos Island specimens, arranging them in a way that shows their differences as well as their similarities. Darwin is becoming more and more aware that changes, however slight, are important in some way.

If the Earth's geology is changing slowly – over very long periods of time – through the action of earthquakes, glaciers, volcanoes and rivers, could plants and animals have changed over time too? Changed to create new types, such as those on the Galápagos Islands?

So many questions! Darwin pays close attention to details that others fail to notice.

THE MYSTERY OF LIFE

Darwin suspects that all living things are linked to a common origin, and he's worked out that the different types probably change over time. But he's yet to discover the mystery of how this happens.

'Show me a tortoise,' Vice Governor Lawson had stated, 'and I'll tell you which island it came from.' Over and over again these words come back to Darwin as he considers the differences between the tortoises. Their size, colour, type of scales and length of legs, as well as the shape of their shells. From thin, easily broken shells, to dome-shaped shells, to thick, elongated shells turned up in the front like Spanish saddles. 'Why?' asks Darwin. 'Why are there different tortoises, finches, mockingbirds and plants for different Galápagos islands?'

DARWIN MOVES HOUSE

When Darwin and Emma Wedgwood decide to marry, Darwin moves to a house at 12 Upper Gower Street. Covington, meanwhile, is starting to make plans of his own. But first he helps Darwin to once again pack and unpack countless boxes of specimens.

The move goes smoothly. With Covington's help, two large horse-drawn vans are loaded with Darwin's specimens, along with a few dozen drawers of shells. Darwin organises one of his rooms as a museum.

Tom, Dick and Harry are the last to be moved to the tall brick house. As Covington gently lifts each giant tortoise into the driftwood box, he says softly, 'You've hardly grown at all. And look at you, Master Harry. Handsome as ever with your dark shell, but only a little bit bigger than when Darwin picked you up on James Island.'

COVINGTON LEAVES
FOR AUSTRALIA

After seven years at Darwin's side, Covington has decided to go his own way. Up in the attic room, he packs his belongings.

So it's a partly sad, partly happy day when Covington leaves

London for his new life in Australia. Holding an excellent reference from Darwin and his emigration papers for Sydney, Covington says a final farewell to the tortoises, and to Darwin. He is about to embark on an exciting new adventure.

Tom, Dick and Harry miss Covington's cheerful chatter, as well as the sound of his fiddle echoing through Darwin's rooms. But Darwin and his new assistant soon fill the gap left by Covington.

GIANT TORTOISES AS LUGGAGE

Three years later, Darwin's friend John Clements Wickham visits 12 Upper Gower Street. Darwin often thinks of Wickham, who was first lieutenant on the *Beagle*. Wickham used to tease Darwin about dumping the slimy contents of his plankton net on the *Beagle*'s spotless decks. But Darwin and Wickham have remained good friends.

Darwin invites Wickham to step outside into the long, narrow garden at the back of Darwin's house. One part of the neatly clipped lawn is reserved for the giant tortoises. While watching them graze half-heartedly, Wickham observes, 'They don't seem to be all that interested in eating.'

'I'm sure that the soot on the grass ruins its taste,' says Darwin, 'even though I try to rinse it away. But their appetite for fruit and vegetables is also poor. Although they're surviving, they're not thriving. I'm worried about them. Whenever I put myself in Harry's shoes, I want to live in a warmer place, where the air is clean and the vegetation crisp and unpolluted.'

'You've done well to keep them alive these past five years,' remarks Wickham. 'Most tropical animals die during their first winter in this climate. But I've got an idea. Would you like me to take them to Australia?'

'What part of Australia do you have in mind?'

'I've been offered the position of police magistrate in the new settlement of Moreton Bay (later known as the city of Brisbane). It's a semi-tropical coastal region with a similar climate to that of the Galápagos Islands.'

Darwin squats down beside Harry and runs his fingers lightly over the tortoise's shell. Then, while examining the smears of soot colouring his fingertips, Darwin remarks sadly, 'The tortoises are in trouble. This cold, smoky atmosphere is no good for them. I'll be sorry to see them go, but I very much fear they'll die if they remain in London.

'I've studied them for five years,' he continues to his friend, 'and they haven't grown much since I collected them. So the two boxes that Covington made should be big enough to ship them to Australia. They're stored in the basement.'

The men step indoors again and sit in Darwin's study on the ground floor. As they wait for tea, sandwiches and cake to be served, Wickham becomes absorbed in Darwin's beetle collection, while Darwin thinks back to the Galápagos Islands.

Tom, Dick and Harry – each one collected from a different island – are now showing small differences. Harry's shell is slightly more domed and is a darker colour. Tom's shell is smaller, while Dick's legs are a little longer, and his neck reaches up a little higher. Dick also has one pale-coloured claw. The plates making up the tortoises' shells are starting to vary too. Different islands, different tortoises.

'An island in the sun. A new home in a much warmer place,' murmurs Darwin, as a maid brings in the afternoon tea. 'Yes. I'll take up your offer with grateful thanks.'

Out in the garden again, as the two men make plans to transport the tortoises, Harry raises his head to look up into their eyes. He can sense change again; another journey is about to begin. Tom gives a wide yawn. Dick merely continues to breathe.

CHAPTER 3
Relaxing in sub-tropical Australia

The return voyage to Australia is, for the giant tortoises, more comfortable than their journey from the Galápagos Islands to London. The trio adapts quickly to life on board another sailing ship. They are steering towards a new life in a new country.

Up and down, down and up. The movement of the sailing ship lulls Harry into a kind of dream. He sees clouds drifting across the sky, and through cracks in the box, the shimmering sea. Stars whisper secrets to the moon. A gull's shadow passes over the box. Wind plays in the sails. Harry feels as if he'll float forever in the oceans dividing England from Australia.

After sailing for a little over three months, the ship glides into a safe anchorage close to the new settlement of Brisbane. The year is 1842.

Shortly after his arrival in Brisbane, John Wickham marries Anna Macarthur, and the tortoises move in with the newly-wed couple. Anna is the daughter of a famous pioneer wool grower, so she's grown up surrounded by animals. She isn't bothered one bit by Wickham's pet tortoises.

'Other people have cats and dogs,' boasts Anna to dinner guests, 'whereas we have three Galápagos giant tortoises!'

After the chill of England, Tom, Dick and Harry welcome the balmy warmth of Queensland. Unable to regulate their body temperature, they need the heat from the sun to warm their bodies. Australia's sunshine is perfect.

Harry sees the Brisbane River snaking its way through the bushland. He feels at home in the steamy heat. The sunshine warms his bones and he feels a surge of happiness. No longer does he need to spend so much time sheltering beneath his shell.

BACK IN ENGLAND, DARWIN'S BOOK HITS THE STANDS

In 1859, after many, many years of secrecy, Charles Darwin reveals his controversial theory of evolution in a book he calls *The Origin of Species*. This book is considered the most important biological work ever written.

In his book, Darwin puts forward three main points. Firstly, that today's plants and animals have developed from earlier forms through a process called natural selection or the 'survival of the fittest'. Secondly, that all living things form part of the single web of life. And thirdly, that in order to survive, most species change over time.

DARWIN'S OBSESSION ABOUT DIFFERENCES

Ever since 1835, Darwin has been obsessed by the small differences he sees between plants and animals of the same type (or species).

Undoubtedly, the plants and animals of the Galápagos Islands (including Tom, Dick and Harry) led Darwin to the realisation that these slight differences form the building blocks of evolution. Charles Darwin's understanding of the origins of life on Earth earn him the title of 'genius'.

BUT BACK TO HARRY IN QUEENSLAND

In 1860, John Wickham decides to retire from his demanding position as first government resident, and return to England.

The tortoises have been in his care for 18 years, and he has become very attached to them. He is concerned about their future and wants them to have a happy home amongst people who care for them properly.

After much thought, Wickham approaches the management at the Brisbane Botanic Gardens and offers to donate the three tortoises to the Gardens. With some sadness, he delivers Tom, Dick and Harry to their new home.

The night before he is due to set sail for England, Wickham visits the Botanic Gardens to bid the tortoises one last farewell. He whispers, 'Farewell, my friends. I'm sorry to leave you, but you're in good hands. There are two keepers who will look after you, and I know you'll like living here in the Gardens. If I took you back to England you'd die, and no one wants that to happen.'

LIVING IN THE BRISBANE BOTANIC GARDENS

The tortoises' new enclosure in the Brisbane Botanic Gardens is spacious, with lots of room for them to exercise. There's a pool of water, palm trees for shade, and plenty of grass to eat.

While Tom and Dick concentrate on eating, Harry sets off to

explore the boundaries. Soon Harry meets up with the small herd of deer that share the enclosure. But one look at Harry and the deer panic. Never before have they seen such a prehistoric-looking creature!

'How strange!' thinks Harry. 'At the smallest sign of danger, the deer run off to the other side of the enclosure. They are so nervous that they panic first and think later. If I'm scared, I just tuck my head beneath my shell.'

In the same year that Wickham leaves Australia, Tom, Dick and Harry turn 30 years of age. But their birthday is neither recognised nor celebrated. Although the keepers take good care of the tortoises, they don't think that tortoises have or need birthdays. So there is no birthday cake. No candles. No presents.

ARE THEY MALES OR FEMALES?

Although the trio is named Tom, Dick and Harry, no one in Brisbane knows for sure how to recognise whether they're male or female. In fact, no one knows much at all about Galápagos giant tortoises. If they are male and female, they're old enough to have mated with one another, to produce eggs, then hatchlings. But maybe they haven't bred because they are all the same sex? All male. Or all female.

'The climate should be ideal,' says one of the keepers to the other, 'and their diet is varied enough, so if there is a male and a female, they should have bred by now.'

'That's if their enclosure is big enough,' replies the other keeper. 'Perhaps they don't get enough exercise, or even enough privacy? Maybe that's why they haven't bred.'

Tom and Dick are not the slightest bit interested in the debate. But Harry's eyes twinkle with the secret.

AND THEN THERE WERE TWO

By the late 1800s, only two of the three Galápagos giant tortoises remain. No one ever establishes the cause of Dick's death. One day he is alive. The next he is dead. When the keeper discovers the body, he turns Dick over onto his back. He certainly looks very strange on his back, but there is no sign of injury or disease. The keeper wonders whether Dick has simply died of old age. He feels a little sad but knows that he'd be a lot more upset if it was Harry who had died. Harry is his favourite.

As each of the Galápagos giant tortoises lives in a world of his own, linked more closely to their keeper than to one another, Harry doesn't pay much attention to Dick's death. Perhaps their lack of closeness to one another is because as young tortoises they were handled so much by Covington. Therefore they bond more closely to humans than they do to other tortoises.

To this day, nobody knows where Dick is buried.

BRISBANE RIVER
BURSTS ITS BANKS

Tom and Harry breathe in the hot humid air, tasting it with their nostrils, predicting rain. And their feeling about the weather is accurate to the day. It begins with a rumble of thunder, followed closely by a torrential downpour. Then the rain seems to forget how to stop. The date is February 1893.

Day after day of continuous rain hammers Dick and Harry's shells. The Brisbane River bursts its banks. Eleven people drown, two bridges are swept away and flood debris floats into Brisbane's central business district. People are evacuated as rising flood waters swirl along city streets, flooding homes, turning streets into rivers. The rain goes on and on.

Historical documents are destroyed, including some records

of the three giant tortoises between the years 1842 and 1893.

One of the keepers begins to worry about the safety of the animals within the enclosure, so he cuts through one side of the fence then herds the deer and giant tortoises to drier ground. Galápagos giant tortoises are land animals and cannot swim like sea turtles. Harry takes the lead, while Tom trails behind, shuffling slowly.

Munching on leaves heavy with moisture, the giant tortoises watch as the gun-boat *Paluma* rises on the swollen river and beaches itself in the Botanic Gardens. Fourteen days later, Harry watches as a wall of water floats the gun-boat back into the Brisbane River, as if it had never moved! Thirty degrees Celsius, combined with heavy rain doesn't make for comfortable conditions. But Tom and Harry are experts at adapting to difficulties. They'll survive this crisis.

AN ALL-OVER MUD BATH

Tom and Harry look particularly handsome with their shells washed clean by the rain. No more bird droppings. No more dust. Their shiny shells seem brand new, even though they are 63 years old. And the surrounding vegetation sparkles as well.

Whenever they can, Tom and Harry soak in the muddy pools

within the Gardens. Buzzing flies, and clouds of whining mosquitoes and sandflies are enough to drive any creature crazy. But a layer of mud all over gives the giant tortoises some protection from these annoying and blood-sucking insects. The pond water cools them as well.

At night the tortoises sleep to the sounds of trilling, chirping, wailing, tinkling frogs. Frogs that sing their melodies against the silence of the star-studded sky.

GETTING HUNGRY

Tom and Harry's food supply is becoming less and less appetising. Because of the flood, the flowers are limp and water-sodden, and the grass tastes of mud. Everything smells foul and rotten. Tom and Harry lumber slowly up the slope, searching beneath the thick canopy of trees for more tasty food. Their keeper notices that Harry is finding food and shelter for both himself and Tom. So at this stage, the keeper doesn't worry about the giant tortoises. In any case, the staff at the Botanic Gardens are busy trying to save the rare and precious plants in their care.

After the 1893 flood, several short, sharp bursts of rain cleanse the grass on which Tom and Harry graze. Once more they munch happily, cutting the fresh grass neatly between their knife-sharp jaws. By three o'clock in the afternoon, though, their eyelids become heavy and they burrow into a nest of leaves beneath the dense canopy of a fig tree. They love their afternoon nap. Life is simple. Life is good again.

A LIVING MUSEUM

Meanwhile, Brisbane's Botanic Gardens have become a zoological gardens as well. With wide, curious eyes Harry watches while men in overalls build animal cages, aviaries and enclosures. 'What are the cages for?' wonders Harry.

The following day, two bears arrive at the Gardens. Harry stretches out his neck to get a better view of these strange creatures. A few days later, monkeys and koalas arrive. Then flamingos, finches and a rare New Zealand kea. By now, Tom is curious as well. The two Galápagos giant tortoises spend many hours each day observing the new animals. Harry enjoys watching the monkeys leap about their cage, swinging by their tails. Tom prefers the two woolly bears.

As the years pass, the giant tortoises grow, little by little. Soon they are the size of small tables. Hot, steamy summers merge into the clear blue skies and warm sunny days of winter.

LOVING CHILDREN

Now that the Botanic Gardens have also become a zoo, children are regular visitors. Tom and Harry learn to love children. Harry, in particular, enjoys the affection they show him. He likes to have his neck patted, and to feel children's arms around his shell. He loves it when they look into his eyes and tell him their deepest secrets.

Every afternoon, the keeper helps a few children pick bunches of brightly coloured flowers to feed the tortoises. Many of the flowers and leaves in the Botanic and Zoological Gardens are poisonous so the keeper teaches the children which leaves and flowers to select. They must never feed the tortoises oleanders, poppies, iris, azaleas or daffodils. These plants could kill Harry and Tom or at least cause diarrhoea, blindness, or heart troubles. Hibiscus flowers and chestnut leaves, though, are considered safe and get a big thumbs-up from the tortoises.

AND THEN THERE WAS ONE

In 1929, Tom, who has been Harry's companion for 94 years, dies quite suddenly. One day he's behaving normally, but the following day he doesn't emerge from his pile of leaves. Two of the keepers pull Tom's body out from beneath the bedding.

'He's dead,' says the head keeper, bending down to touch the stiffened neck.

'You're right,' agrees the other keeper. 'As dead as a dodo. It'll be strange with just one tortoise. But Harry'll be okay. He's never taken much notice of Tom. Harry's much more interested in you!'

Harry, who's been out grazing, comes lumbering over and reaches out his neck for the head keeper to stroke. As the man caresses the folds, he asks, 'Do you think Harry knows that Tom is dead?'

'I bet he does. I can't be sure what goes on in that head, but I suspect Harry knows a lot more than we give him credit for. But what are we going to do about the body?'

'The Queensland Museum may be interested,' says the head keeper. 'I'll get in touch with them straightaway. They have the expertise to preserve his body. At least this way Tom will have a place amongst other rare and endangered creatures. He will be preserved and people will be able to see him for centuries to come.'

'And we won't have to dig a hole to bury him in,' observed the other keeper, with relief.

No one ever establishes the cause of Tom's death. He becomes an exhibit at the Queensland Museum but a mistake is made and he's labelled as an Aldabra tortoise, a different species of giant tortoise living on Aldabra Island in the Indian Ocean. As a result, his identity is lost for 65 years.

MEETING THE PLATYPUS MAN

In early 1939 Harry has an important visitor. Not the kind of visitor who is greeted with a red carpet, brass band and finely dressed dignitaries. David Fleay comes quietly, as an ordinary person passing through Brisbane. But David Fleay is far from ordinary. In actual fact, he's on his way to New Guinea, where he plans to collect and study animals native to that country. Visiting the Brisbane Botanic and Zoological Gardens is an extra treat.

Within five minutes of walking through the gate, David Fleay comes face to face with Harry. David has heard about Harry but is overwhelmed by the sight of the giant tortoise's calm, friendly face.

'Some day,' he says, 'I'd like you to live with me. I don't know how this will come about. I only know that it will happen.'

Harry shuffles forward to meet David. Stretching out his wrinkly neck, he sniffs David's pocket. 'I wasn't expecting you to be interested in banana,' says David, laughing. 'That was supposed to be a treat for the monkeys. But what they don't know, they won't miss, will they, my friend?'

Harry savours the taste of the ripe banana, chewing it for a very long time. He too feels a connection with this twinkly-eyed man. He trusts him, and senses that some time, maybe in the distant future, their paths will meet again.

DAVID FLEAY'S ENCOUNTER WITH A TASMANIAN TIGER

In a flower garden nearby, a gardener says to the head keeper, 'That's David Fleay talking to Harry. I've heard he was the last person to be bitten by the now extinct Tasmanian Tiger.'

'You mean that wolf-like marsupial, the last of its kind, which was housed at the Hobart Domain Zoo?'

'Yes,' replies the gardener with a chuckle, as he pulls out some weeds, 'apparently David, while researching and photographing the animal in 1933, was given a painful nip on his backside!'

'David Fleay was also the first person to "milk" a taipan, one of the world's deadliest snakes,' continues the head keeper. 'They use the "milk" to produce life-saving antivenene.'

KING OF THE GARDENS

Seasons change, the Brisbane River rises and falls, years drift by. Gradually, the area containing bird aviaries, cages of monkeys, deer and antelopes disappear as animals either die or are relocated. From the iron-rail fence it is no longer possible to view captive birds and animals.

Meanwhile, Harry goes from living within an enclosure to living free within the Botanic and Zoological Gardens. He loves the choices that are now open to him. During the great flood of 1893, and for a while afterwards, he remembers being free like this, only now there's no muddy water polluting his food.

Harry is king of the Gardens.

'He's like the Pied Piper,' says the head keeper to a mother of two small children. 'Look at all those children trailing him wherever he wanders. Oh, to be so popular!'

Across sweeping lawns and along sandy pathways the children follow, with the giant tortoise always on the lookout for tasty morsels to eat. Mulberry and loquat leaves are vacuumed up, but the children keep the tortoise away from the kitchen garden, where the poisonous leaves of potato and rhubarb could harm their hero.

'Look at him now!' exclaims the mother to her toddlers. 'It seems Harry is about to go for a swim.'

Hanging on tightly to her children's hands, she watches for a while, then continues, 'Harry is following his favourite pathway down to that lovely pond, floating with lily pads. Harry is thinking of cool, clean water and is looking forward to an all-over soak. But I don't want you joining Harry amongst the lily pads, because you can't swim yet.'

'Actually,' says the head keeper, 'Harry can't swim either. But it's over 30 degrees Celsius, so he's hot, just like us. Giant tortoises aren't swimmers, like sea turtles, so you watch him carefully and make sure he stays in shallow water!'

FLOWERS GET HARRY INTO BIG TROUBLE

'No!' shouts the new gardener, running towards a freshly weeded flower bed, 'Get out of my garden!'

But Harry is too interested in the feast of rose petals, nasturtiums, frangipanis, blue monkey-tails, daisies and violets to take any notice of the gardener's cries.

'You're like a herd of stampeding cattle!' he yells, waving his angry fists at Harry as the tortoise enters another garden and plucks pansies, orchids and cactus flowers, then smashes through the greenery with his heavy shell.

Harry knows that he needs to eat a wide variety of leaves, buds, fruits and flowers – even if the gardeners think otherwise!

To Harry, this oasis of colour is irresistible.

Life is good in this environment of green, closely clipped lawns, large shady trees, clumps of bamboo and ornamental lakes teaming with fish. 'Why,' Harry wonders, 'do humans continue to work in the middle of the day, especially in the sticky, humid heat of summer?' He sees their stressed, unhappy faces and feels sad that they can't relax.

With curiosity, Harry watches people jogging through the Gardens and wonders, 'Why do they push themselves so hard, rush around at such a hectic pace?'

Harry, of course, is the living expert of the slow and steady pace. And throughout the hottest part of the day he does what all sensible creatures do. He rests in a cool place.

Ferries chug lazily up and down the river, loaded with tourists who are enjoying the scenic river cruise. And along the riverbank visiting yachts are moored, attracted by the palm trees, sunshine and balmy weather.

GRAFFITI OF THE WORST KIND

During this time, when Harry roams free within the Gardens, vandals climb the fence one night. Despite the full moon which floods the Gardens in a pale light, it's difficult to see Harry who is resting beside a pile of raked up leaves.

Instinctively Harry knows that these people sneaking around in the moonlight are up to no good. So he keeps very, very still. But they find him anyway. 'There he is!' one of the gang exclaims, 'over there beside the bamboo!'

Harry flinches as he feels the pen knife carving into his shell. He tries to escape into a patch of lush tropical vegetation, but the gang follows and they block his way. Tucking his head beneath his shell is his only defence. So the carving continues until each member of the gang is satisfied.

Initials carved into rock look ugly. But initials engraved into a giant tortoise's shell is unbelievably cruel. How did they not realise that carving their initials was harming Harry, especially when they noticed blood oozing beneath their pen knives?

Harry's shell, made of fused bone, is a combination of ribs, backbone and shoulder bones. Nobody could seriously believe that to cut into bone would be painless. Perhaps the problem is that some people don't think at all.

With their signatures carved into Harry's shell, the culprits clamber over the fence of the Gardens. Shocked and in pain, Harry retreats into the shrubbery and burrows beneath his pile of leaves to sleep off his wounds. He will carry the scars for the rest of his life.

Charles Darwin was kind to humans and animals alike. He would have been horrified by this brutal act.

THE STAR ATTRACTION

People of all ages visit the Brisbane Botanic and Zoological Gardens, and Harry is usually their favourite attraction. People who work in the city often stroll into the Gardens to have their lunch. Often they share their food with him, feeding him banana, strawberries and mangoes.

As humans move from generation to generation, Harry remains a constant presence in the Brisbane Botanic and Zoological Gardens. Time passes, yet Harry is always there.

Grandparents visit him, murmuring softly into his ear, 'I wonder if you remember me, Harry? I stroked you when I was eight years old. Then I visited you again when my own children were young. Now I'm introducing my grandchildren to you. I wonder if you'll still be around to meet my great-grandchildren?'

People remember Harry through the ever-changing colours of each and every season. Young children are lifted up onto his massive shell, and there they ride, like warriors, as Harry takes them along mysterious shaded paths, through dense rainforest, and past exotic flowers. Harry becomes famous for taking toddlers for short piggy-back rides, walking very slowly so they don't fall off. It's difficult to balance when perched high up on Harry's shell! The giant tortoise enjoys the delighted squeals and excited chatter of the children.

But sometimes he wishes the older children weren't so heavy, and that they didn't stay on his back for such long periods of time. And sometimes the sheer number of children wanting a ride overwhelms Harry – and makes him tired. But it doesn't do him any harm, and he loves the attention!

A CIRCUS COMES TO TOWN

Harry feels as though he's joined a circus when, in 1949, a group of elephants, orangutans, gibbons, a honey bear and panther move into his territory. Thousands of visitors come to look at the circus animals quarantined within the Gardens. These animals need to be separated from the other circus animals for a few months, to make sure they don't spread disease.

The circus animals are used to living alongside one another. But Harry feels his territory has been invaded. Especially when the mischievous orangutans pelt Harry with small sticks and stones as he is taking his evening walk past their enclosure.

In response, Harry does what any Galápagos giant tortoise would do. He pulls his head into the protection of his shell and waits until the orangutans have run out of ammunition. Cautiously then, he continues on his walk around the Gardens.

A LOVABLE BULLDOZER

In 1958, the head keeper retires and the management of the Gardens decides to close the zoological part of the Brisbane Botanic Gardens. Because Harry bulldozes his way through the flowerbeds, the manager says, 'Harry must go. He's causing too much damage to the plants and, after all, the Gardens were designed for precious plants and trees – not Galápagos giant tortoises.'

After living in the Brisbane Botanic Gardens for 98 years, the tortoise is about to be sent away. Harry faces an uncertain future.

'Don't worry, Harry,' says the head keeper reassuringly, 'I'm sure we'll find you a good home. In fact, I've just had an idea. I've only now remembered a man with a fauna park who always asks after you. I'll phone him right now.'

In Australia, Harry's lived through cyclones, droughts, floods, bushfires and violent storms. Harry is a survivor. He is soon to meet up with an old friend.

CHAPTER 4
Adventures with the Platypus Man

One hundred and twenty-eight years is a grand old age for any creature. For Harry it marks the beginning of a new era.

On a fine sunny day in 1958, a Ford truck pulls up alongside the Brisbane Botanic Gardens and out steps a very excited David Fleay. For 19 years the zoologist has waited for an opportunity to purchase the Galápagos giant tortoise. With his own fauna reserve on Queensland's Gold Coast up and running, David Fleay is keen to load the rare, table-sized tortoise into his small truck, then take Harry home to West Burleigh Heads, south of Brisbane.

'Hello, Harry, my friend!' exclaims David, as he approaches the tortoise. 'I'm so pleased to see you, but even more happy that I'll be taking you home with me.'

Running his hand lightly over Harry's neck, David continues, 'And you remember me too. I'm sure of that. I've waited for this opportunity for a very long time. I promise I'll take good care of you.'

Alert dark eyes gaze back at David in recognition. Harry presses his neck into David's hand, asking for more stroking.

With help from the head keeper and three gardeners, David lifts Harry up into the back of the truck where the giant tortoise is lowered carefully onto a bed of hay. Harry isn't frightened. He trusts these hands that lift him up and into the vehicle. It reminds Harry of early days when, as a five-year-old, he was picked up by Charles Darwin and loaded aboard the *Beagle*.

A HOME IN A RAINFOREST

Nestled in the foothills of West Burleigh Heads, surrounded by lush rainforest, David Fleay's sanctuary is home to many rare and endangered species. David's emphasis is on education, scientific research and the conservation of endangered species through captive breeding programs. He approaches his work with a sensitive understanding and passion for all animals – but especially for Harry.

David Fleay thinks back to 1944 when he was the first person to breed platypus in captivity. He thinks of the platypus parents, Jack and Jill, and of their baby he called Corrie. Then, of taking a pair of breeding platypus to the New York Zoo, where he helped the Americans design and build the first platypusary in the United States.

SPREADING NEWS OF HARRY FAR AND WIDE

As a writer, David Fleay spreads news of Harry all over Australia, and overseas as well. Never in a hurry and never shy, Harry is an instant favourite with the many Australian and international tourists who visit Fleay's Fauna Reserve. Harry has time to 'talk', using his loud, raspy voice to greet visitors. Harry has time to spend with anyone who loves animals. He happily poses for photographs, especially when carrying small children on his back. Sometimes he carries three young children at one time.

The Galápagos giant tortoise is fortunate to have the freedom of several large grassy areas, sharing his space with kangaroos and wallabies, as well as wild lizards and birds. When an agile wallaby tries to steal his carrot, lettuce or celery,

Harry hisses loudly. On other days, however, he allows his friend to share the meal. Harry relishes his daily fruit and vegetable salad.

FLIES CAN DRIVE ANYONE CRAZY

Bush flies add to the sounds of the bush, and torment humans and animals alike with their annoying persistence. Harry doesn't like flies. They use his shell for a free ride and, looking for food and moisture, constantly buzz around his eyes, nose and mouth. Until a friend of his arrives – a small black and white willie wagtail bird, named Willie.

With an insatiable appetite for sticky black bush flies, the willie wagtail is a welcome friend. And not only because he eats annoying flies.

'Sweet pretty creature,' sings Willie, as he performs clever aerobatics around Harry.

But there's a darker side to Willie. Jealousy. Whenever any other bird tries to befriend Harry, Willie utters a harsh chattering call, while at the same time raising his white eyebrows and puffing out his black throat. Then, from his perch high up on Harry's shell, he chases away the intruder.

By slashing figures of eight in the air, and making rapid passes behind his rival's neck, Willie manages to drive away the competition. Returning to Harry's shell, a self-satisfied Willie fans his tail feathers, preens his glossy plumage then recommences duties as chief flycatcher.

HARRY BECOMES HARRIET!

One day Paul Breese, the director of the Honolulu Zoo in Hawaii, visits Fleay's Fauna Reserve. He makes an important discovery.

Paul specialises in Galápagos giant tortoises, and has managed to breed them in captivity – a difficult process.

'Have you got a car jack handy?' he asks David, running his fingers over Harry's strong back legs. 'I'd like to take a look beneath his shell, to check that he really is a male.'

From a white Holden ute parked nearby, David Fleay takes a jack and passes it to Paul saying, 'I have to admit that everyone, including myself, has just assumed that Harry's a male. Nobody's had the expertise to say otherwise.'

Paul places the steel jack under Harry's shell, between the giant tortoise's hind legs then says, 'If you can talk to him, David, and stay by his head, that should calm him while we raise his rear end. And,' continues Paul, gesturing to a couple of men working nearby, 'if you guys could stand on either side, to steady him, that would be a great help.'

As Paul winds up the jack, Harry's weight begins to transfer from his hind legs to his front legs. 'It's okay,' says David Fleay, in a crooning voice. As David strokes Harry's neck, he continues, 'We just want to check out your sex to make sure that your name really should be Harry.'

Feeling decidedly uncomfortable and off balance, Harry squirms a little, wondering what on earth is happening. Never before has anyone done this to him. But if David Fleay says it's okay, then it must be. For Harry trusts David one hundred per cent.

After examining beneath the tortoise's tail and checking out the hollow under the shell, Paul Breese stands up, stretches then says, 'I've got news for you, David. Harry is a female! A male Galápagos giant tortoise has a thicker, longer tail and is more hollowed out beneath its shell than a female. This enables it to mount a female and stay on her back long enough to mate successfully.'

David smiles broadly and says, 'Then the grand old lady's name will be Harriet!'

THE GREAT ESCAPE

By sharing her life with the Fleay family and her wildlife keepers, as well as lizards, snakes, insects, frogs, birds, kangaroos and wallabies, Harriet is never lonely. Occasionally though, she gets it into her head that she wants to return to the Galápagos Islands, half a world away. Could it be that she wants to find a mate and breed baby tortoises?

Harriet is reported missing every now and then. When the mood takes her, she barges through any barrier, whether it's a wire netting fence or pieces of timber held together with nails. Like a bulldozer, she presses her immense weight against anything that stands in her path, until a large hole opens up. Harriet has elephant-like muscles and a very strong will!

One morning, at daybreak, Harriet forces her way through a strongly constructed wire fence. Her toes tingle with the effort of her escape. The sun is just beginning to peep up over the trees, but it's not yet hot. There's shade in the forest but here in the lighter bush, dragonflies swoop about like fairies in the pale blue sky. Harriet enjoys hearing the birds wake up, but there are so many logs, holes and bushes to get past on her way to the Galápagos Islands that she wonders how many days it'll take before she arrives at her destination. Harriet is thinking about making babies. Not about poisonous snakes. Not about crocodiles. Not about crossing the Pacific Ocean.

It's winter, so the ground is hard and dry. Trampling over leaves, sticks, fallen logs and dead grass is difficult work. They crackle and crunch beneath her feet. As Harriet drags her shell over an ant mound, tiny black ants crawl up her legs. But none of this bothers her. Her mind is fixed on other things!

Fortunately, she doesn't try to cross Tallebudgera Creek. She might've got caught in its tangle of mangrove roots and slushy mud. But she does press on through rough bushland, leaving behind a trail of broken earth, scrub, ferns and grasses. Luckily, prickles and burrs can't puncture her tough, scaly skin. She notices her shadow, dark and bulky, plodding along beside her. Looking up into the trees, she sees glimpses of a pale blue sky.

'Dad! Dad! Harriet's gone!' David's son Stephen yells into the crisp morning air. 'She's broken through the wire fence and I can't see her anywhere!'

David Fleay's sons, Stephen and Robert, along with four of their employees, set out immediately to find Harriet. It's not difficult to follow the trail of broken shrubs, sticks and leaves that mark her progress through the bush. Every now and then, the drag mark of a giant tortoise's shell marks an area of bare earth.

Looking ahead, Robert points then exclaims, 'There she is!' The other men catch a glimpse of the escapee as she disappears behind a clump of wattle trees. Within five minutes though, Harriet is surrounded by a group of very hot and tired men.

'You can't possibly walk all the way across the Pacific Ocean to the Galápagos Islands,' David says, trying to persuade Harriet not to escape again. 'Now let's get going and in no time at all we'll have you back where you belong, eating your breakfast.'

Bringing home the escapee, however, proves a difficult task. Already it's hot and humid.

'When I say lift, could you all please lift?' says David, positioning himself by Harriet's head.

Feeling upset, Harriet grunts and squirms uncomfortably as they lift her up then turn her over and place her upside down in the large wheelbarrow.

'I haven't made it back to the Galápagos Islands, after all,' she thinks sadly. 'On the other hand, though, I'm feeling rather hungry, so maybe I'll go back and have breakfast, then try again when nobody's around.'

With crunchy lettuce and the tangy taste of mangoes on her mind, Harriet stops struggling as the men begin the journey back to the fauna reserve. Some of them push the barrow, while others

make sure Harriet doesn't fall out. Everyone is involved. A giant tortoise in a wheelbarrow is a heavy and very awkward load.

After twenty minutes or so, the men are exhausted. Streaked with dirt, and with sweat trickling down their backs, they puff and pant through a particularly rough stretch of bush, aiming for clearer country ahead.

'She's slipping,' gasps one of the teenagers, 'I'm losing my grip…' Before he can stop himself, he's tripped over a log and fallen headlong into a ditch. Harriet balances precariously, nearly tipping out of the wheelbarrow.

'I'm sorry…' the teenager murmurs in a low exhausted voice, feeling like a fool in front of his hero, David Fleay.

'There's no harm done to Harriet,' says David kindly, 'and it's time to take a break anyway.'

By the time Harriet arrives back in her enclosure, everyone is worn out. Harriet can think only of her breakfast salad, which is ready and waiting for her.

AN UNDIGNIFIED RETURN JOURNEY

An alternative method of bringing Harriet home from her occasional walkabouts involves the use of a tarpaulin or canvas tent fly. She's turned onto her back on the tarpaulin, then dragged back to the fauna reserve by six strong men. Harriet hates this method of rescue even more than the wheelbarrow. Her sighs are loud enough to be heard from far, far away. Harriet's feelings are hurt. Badly. How embarrassing! How undignified! Harriet screws her eyes tightly shut and pretends she is somewhere else.

But dreaming doesn't make the journey on the tarpaulin any more dignified. So, on some occasions, this grand old lady returns through her hole in the fence of her own free will.

When she voluntarily returns from one of her expeditions, she's rewarded with an extra special treat. Hibiscus flowers.

LONESOME GEORGE IN DESPERATE NEED OF A MATE

One evening, while reading a scientific journal, David Fleay discovers that a world-wide search has been launched to find a female Galápagos giant tortoise to breed with Lonesome George, who's almost certainly the last member of his subspecies anywhere in the world.

Putting aside the journal, David says excitedly to his wife

Sigrid, 'Lonesome George is native to the tiny, volcanic island of Pinta, in the Galápagos Islands. In 1971, National Park wardens – who were hunting feral goats – found Lonesome George hiding in the mountains all by himself. He's been lonely for a very long time. Lonesome George is so precious that he's kept at the Charles Darwin Research Station on the island of Santa Cruz. He lives in a captive breeding enclosure, and is protected and cared for like royalty.'

'Is it possible that Harriet could be a Pinta Island tortoise?' asks Sigrid, lifting her head from her newspaper.

'Anything's possible,' says David, leaning back in his chair and adjusting his spectacles.

Then, gazing out into the garden, he thinks about whether Harriet could become Lonesome George's mate. 'What if Harriet turns out to be a Pinta tortoise?' he wonders. 'Could Harriet and Lonesome George "fall in love" and mate successfully? Could Harriet be the key to saving this endangered subspecies of giant tortoise?'

'Not only could Harriet be a Pinta Island tortoise,' David says to Sigrid, 'but a reward of $10,000 is offered to any zoo able to produce a Pinta female. Imagine being able to put that sort of money into our fauna reserve!'

'If Harriet proves to be of the wrong subspecies,' Sigrid says, 'perhaps the research station can supply a mate for Harriet?'

David Fleay cannot wait for morning to come. He needs to carefully record Harriet's measurements, her shell shape and personality details, as well as take photographs. Several days later, he posts the information to the Charles Darwin Research Station in the Galápagos Islands.

WAITING FOR A LETTER

Impatiently, David Fleay waits for a response to his letter of 23 January 1978. A reply comes within ten days. David tears open the envelope, puts on his reading glasses and scans the letter. No, Harriet is not a Pinta tortoise. David, his family and staff are a little disappointed to read that Harriet, being of a different subspecies, will not be able to breed with Lonesome George to produce hatchlings that will save the Pinta tortoises from extinction. Lonesome George is the only known Pinta tortoise in the world. All the other Pinta tortoises have been either killed for their meat and oil, or starved of food because feral goats have stripped the small island of its vegetation.

On the other hand though, David Fleay and his family are also very relieved. Harriet can continue to live in Australia!

DOMES AND SADDLES

According to the Charles Darwin Research Station, Harriet belongs to the dome-shaped group of giant tortoises whereas Lonesome George belongs to the saddle-shaped form. Harriet's type, with its large dome-shaped shell, evolved to suit the higher areas of the Galápagos island where she hatched. She's designed to eat low growing grasses, fallen fruits and cactus pads, and leaves. Lonesome George has a smaller saddle-shaped shell that's raised at the front. He has a small head, a long neck and long legs. His subspecies has evolved to rise up on their front legs, then stretch their neck as far as it can go to reach the tastiest and most nutritious fruits, blossoms and leaves from trees, creeping vines and shrubs. Having a shell of this shape helps Lonesome George to reach up high. So, both Harriet's subspecies and Lonesome George's subspecies have changed over time, and in different ways, so that they can eat the plants and grasses growing on their particular Galápagos island.

The Charles Darwin Research Station cannot supply a mature male as a mate for Harriet. So, rather than have baby tortoises of her own, Harriet will continue with the important work of educating people about conserving the unique Galápagos Island habitat, and Galápagos giant tortoises in particular.

'IT'S SAD TO SEE
AN OLD FRIEND GO'

In 1987, David Fleay signs over his 23 hectare fauna reserve to the people of Queensland, to be managed by the Queensland Parks and Wildlife Service. But a problem develops when the new owners decide to exhibit only animals native to Australia.

'They've decided that Harriet must go,' says David sadly.

'But Harriet's lived with us for 29 years!' exclaims David's daughter, Rosemary. 'Harriet is the oldest known living animal on Earth today. She's lived in Queensland for 145 years! She's been a Queenslander for much longer than any of us.'

'And people come here especially to see Harriet,' says Sigrid. 'They'll be so disappointed to find her gone. Generations of Queenslanders have got to know and love Harriet.'

'She won't want to go,' says Robert, another of David Fleay's sons. 'Harriet will feel upset that we've sent her away.'

David Fleay is Harriet's best mate. So, it's a sad occasion when Harriet leaves her home of almost 30 years and moves to the Queensland Reptile and Fauna Park at Beerwah – now called Australia Zoo. David doesn't want Harriet to go. David's family and staff don't want her to go either. But the authorities have made a decision and they're not about to change it.

ROBIN STEWART

'You'll have a good home at Australia Zoo,' David whispers into Harriet's ear. Feeling her soft breath on his cheek, he continues, 'I wouldn't let you go unless I was certain you'd be well cared for and appreciated. But I'm getting old now and it's time to say goodbye.'

On the day of her departure, there is sadness and many tears. Because Harriet is so popular, newspaper reporters and even TV cameras record the occasion and hundreds of people come to see her off.

As large as a billiard table and as heavy as an anchor, Harriet can't frolic like a puppy or a lamb. But she loves being the centre of attention, so she rises to the occasion by showing off to a group of young children. Then she nibbles at the TV cameras. Finally, in her raspy voice, which she uses only on special occasions, she bids an affectionate farewell to the Fleay family and staff.

Long after Harriet leaves Fleay's Fauna Reserve, visitors ask her whereabouts. 'We've come,' they say, 'especially to see Harriet.'

Generations of Queenslanders are learning that she now lives in another part of Queensland, on the Sunshine Coast. One zoo's loss is another's gain.

CHAPTER 5

Life at Australia Zoo

Newspapers throughout Australia print the headlines: *Harriet heads off for a new start in life; Famous Galápagos tortoise moves north; Harriet retires to the Sunshine Coast.*

Once again Harriet is on the road, on her way to a new home. As she settles into the deep nest of hay lining the back of the truck, she drifts into a sea of travel memories. Of sailing ships, horse-drawn coaches and trucks.

Bypassing Brisbane on her way to Queensland's Sunshine Coast, Harriet begins to feel a little sad. She is sorry to be leaving David Fleay and his family after 29 happy years. But David has promised he'll visit, and that Australia Zoo will care for her like royalty. Harriet knows that David Fleay always keeps his word.

In 1835, Charles Darwin took over the care of Harriet. In 1842, Captain John Wickham brought Harriet to Australia and looked after her. In 1958, the celebrity naturalist David Fleay became her guardian. Now, in the early 21st century, Australia Zoo is responsible for this extraordinarily precious creature.

Forty minutes' drive north of Brisbane, in an area known as Beerwah, the truck begins to slow down, then turns into a side road on the way to Australia Zoo. Peering through cracks in the side of the truck, Harriet notices the spectacular volcanic peaks of the Glass House Mountains. She doesn't know that they were formed about 25 million years ago. Nor does she know that Captain James Cook gave them this name because they reminded him of glass manufacturing houses back in England.

Slowing down to a crawl, the truck goes past the car park, then along a narrow road and stops beside a spacious enclosure. It's still very early in the morning.

Six strong men are waiting to welcome Harriet to her new home. It takes them about ten minutes to lift her carefully from the truck to the ground within her enclosure. No one wants to risk dropping Harriet because a cracked shell is a serious condition for any tortoise, especially a giant tortoise. Especially an old, precious giant tortoise like Harriet.

'On the count of three,' says the most senior keeper, 'let's lift!'

'One, two, three. Up we go. Boy, what a weight. All 180 kilograms of her!'

Harriet is hoisted up into the air. But she doesn't feel like a bird! In fact, she feels as heavy as an anchor. Trying to get her feet on the ground again, she paddles her legs. But they don't connect. 'It's a bit like being at sea,' she thinks, 'as if I'm on the *Beagle* again.'

'Watch out for that stump, mate,' warns a keeper, 'the last thing we want is to drop her.'

Harriet tilts her head, gazing upwards until her neck begins to ache. So she lowers it and examines the ground instead.

With Harriet's shell clasped firmly between his fingers, the boss keeper says, 'Keep her coming in my direction. Not far to go now. Just a few more metres. Okay, let's lower her now.'

Harriet feels herself coming back to earth. She starts moving her legs again, and this time they touch the ground. As she settles herself and blinks in the strong sunlight, she feels connected again. Part of the earth. 'There you go, Harriet,' says a keeper. 'Welcome to your new home.'

Exploring her new territory, Harriet finds a walk-through

pool, then a rocky cave, with hay bedding and a heater inside. There is a pile of dry leaves beneath a tree, some boulders and a few more trees whose leaves create dark and lighter areas of shade. Harriet's toes sink into the grass as she takes a mouthful of the fresh green blades. Chewing slowly, she realises that if she wants some privacy, she can hide in her environment simply by being still. The leaves and boulders in her enclosure provide her with the perfect camouflage.

Sunshine falls from a pale blue sky, creating pools of light within the enclosure. Perfect for a sun-loving Galápagos giant tortoise. Some people might think it strange that docile, friendly Harriet lives amongst large and very dangerous crocodiles, dragons, deadly snakes and enormous pythons. But don't forget, Harriet is a reptile as well.

The hours of travel have made Harriet weary; she decides to have a rest. She buries herself in the pile of dry leaves and settles into a deep sleep.

A couple of hours later, she feels refreshed, so she rises up on her four stumpy elephant-like legs. Slowly, she walks over to a group of visitors standing alongside the low fence. Her small inquisitive eyes pass quickly over their faces.

They marvel at her huge shell, a shell about the size of a

medium-sized table. They watch as Harriet begins to plod slowly along her sandy pathway.

Early the next day, while munching a mouthful of crisp lettuce, Harriet catches a glimpse of something strange from the corner of her eye. Twisting her long, wrinkly neck over her shell she sees Aldabra giant tortoises in the enclosure next door, and more over the other side of the visitor pathway. 'Thank goodness they haven't put any tortoises in with me,' she thinks. 'I don't like other tortoises. People are much more interesting.'

THE GLOOM SETS IN

As the days blend into weeks and weeks into months, Harriet starts to feel sad. Like a sea fog, a gloominess settles over her. It's so heavy and thick, she wonders whether it will ever disappear. Her keepers are kind, happy people. But Harriet's feeling of sadness is taking the sunshine from her eyes. Blocking her ears to the sound of laughter.

She's missing her friend David Fleay, and every day her sense of loss and sadness increases.

She's too tired to lift up her shell and walk. She retreats within herself. Closes up. Feels empty inside. It's as if all the colour is draining out of her eyes, leaving behind only black and white.

A part of Harriet seems to have died.

THERE'S NOTHING LIKE AN OLD FRIEND

As she always does, Harriet scans the crowd for familiar faces. She looks through the sunhats and sunglasses to the people within. She seems to be searching.

Suddenly, a flash of recognition! She sees someone approaching the fence. She focuses her full attention on him. It's her old friend David Fleay!

A wildlife keeper enters the enclosure with David. 'Here's Harriet,' she says. 'And it sure looks like she remembers you!'

'Hello, my lovely Harriet,' says David, his voice tight with emotion as he reaches forward and holds out his arms to the giant tortoise. 'I can see you're being cared for like a princess.'

David Fleay's words float around Harriet on a gentle breeze. She rubs her wrinkly neck against David's outstretched hands and voices her special raspy welcome. Then, taking a deep breath, she lets herself relax. She feels the sad, misty fog evaporate. Harriet becomes her usual happy self again.

'My children, grandchildren, great-grandchildren and great, great-grandchildren will visit you here,' David says softly to Harriet. 'They'll come from all over Australia to visit you.'

'How many years have you known Harriet?' asks the keeper.

'Forty-nine years.'

'That's a very long time.'

'When I'm no longer of this world, Harriet, you'll be having visits from my family,' says David Fleay.

THE TURNING POINT

David Fleay's visit marks the turning point for Harriet. She begins to see colour again. Golden rays of sunshine. The colourful hats and T-shirts of her visitors. Lush, tropical vegetation. Brilliant flashes of red, blue and green as rainbow lorikeets screech and chatter in the treetops.

BIRTHDAY CELEBRATIONS

On 15 November of every year, Australia Zoo celebrates Harriet's birthday. This particular date is chosen because this is the day when most Galápagos giant tortoises hatch from their eggs.

Harriet's special birthday celebrations take place within her spacious enclosure. Busloads of local school children join in with Australia Zoo staff, volunteer keepers and hundreds of other visitors to celebrate Harriet's big day. Children arrive with bunches of colourful flowers, ready for a party with a difference. The large birthday cake – sometimes as big as Harriet! – with green icing on top, is decorated with flowers. Sometimes Harriet even wears a party hat.

Rising to the occasion, Harriet barges straight through her cake to reach the flowers! She chomps them up, and everyone claps and cheers and sings 'Happy Birthday' to Harriet.

After the cake and the singing, all the visitors want to pat Harriet. But because there are so many people, this is impossible. A few lucky children do, however, have the opportunity. Television cameras and journalists busily record the event, and countless photos are taken. Without doubt, Harriet is one of the most popular and most photographed animals in the world. She is a true celebrity.

Harriet loves to help people celebrate their birthday. Children especially love to share their birthdays with Harriet. But so do older people. One year, a 103-year-old lady chose to visit Harriet on her birthday. Photographs were taken of the two old ladies celebrating in sunny Queensland, both of them

tanned and wrinkled by the Queensland sun. But there hasn't been anyone yet who is as old as Harriet – she is 175 years old!

Harriet's healthy vegetarian diet, combined with a happy and stress-free lifestyle, hold the promise that she will live long into the future – even reaching her 200th birthday.

THE *GUINNESS BOOK OF WORLD RECORDS:* WILL HARRIET MAKE IT?

Although Harriet is the oldest known living animal on Earth today, she isn't the oldest living animal ever recorded in the *Guinness Book of World Records.* That honour goes to a giant tortoise from the Seychelles Islands. In 1766, this tortoise was captured by the French explorer Chevalier de Fresne and presented to the army garrison at Mauritius – an island off the east coast of Africa. The old male tortoise died in 1918 and was thought to be approximately 180 years old.

Another contender for the title of the oldest living animal ever recorded is a Madagascar tortoise called Tu'imalilia. (Madagascar is a large island off the east coast of Africa.) Captain James Cook presented this giant tortoise to the Tongan Royal Family in 1777. The people of Tonga thought so highly of the tortoise that they treated it as a chief. As a result, special keepers cared for it in the grounds of the royal palace. When it died in 1966, Tu'imalilia was believed to be 193 years old.

With Australia Zoo's expert care, do you believe that Harriet will exceed 193 years of age, thereby securing her place in the *Guinness Book of World Records*?

THE SECRET OF HARRIET'S LONG LIFE

Huge and heavy, Harriet does everything slowly. Plods slowly along her pathways, eats her half-bucket of food slowly, blinks slowly, does her droppings slowly. She doesn't like to rush. Sleeping, grazing and basking in the sun are her favourite things to do. Harmony is her motto, a peaceful happiness that spills over all who love her.

Harriet doesn't fret about the past or the future. She lives in the moment. Takes time to smell, listen, look, taste and feel. She lives to the full, within her environment, no matter where life takes her.

Until she reaches 200 years and beyond.

The Hare and the Tortoise: a Fable

Written in the sixth century BC, Aesop's fable of the hare and the tortoise suggests why tortoises live to such a great age.

Long ago a hare was making fun of a tortoise, because the tortoise was moving so slowly.

Instead of getting upset, the wise old tortoise said to the hare, 'I challenge you to a race. We'll soon find out who's the fastest.' The hare snickered with surprise. Nevertheless, he replied, 'Okay. It's stupid but I've got nothing to lose.'

The race began, but the hare was soon so far ahead that he decided to have a rest. He fell into a deep, deep sleep.

The tortoise didn't rest; instead, he plodded steadily on and on and on. After quite a long time, the tortoise reached the finishing line. At that very instant, the hare woke up and began to bound rapidly towards his goal.

But the tortoise had already reached the finishing line.

As we can see with Harriet, slow and steady wins the race!

Find Out More

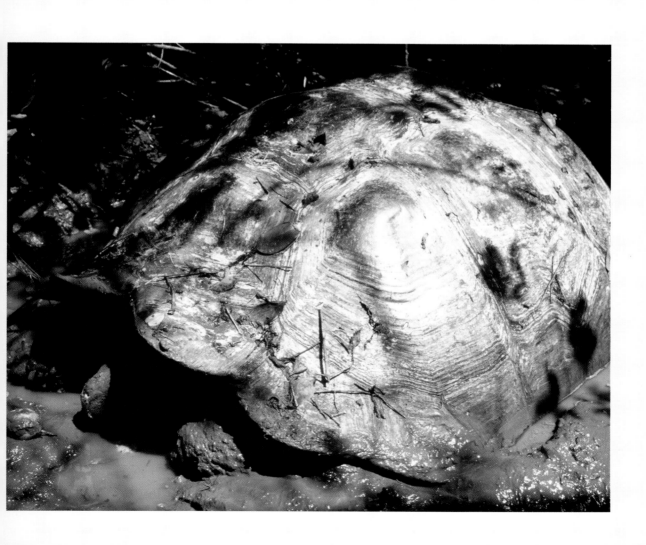

(previous page) Wallowing in her mud bath protects Harriet from mosquitoes and sandflies. *Courtesy of Australia Zoo*

(top) Only Harriet knows the exact details of her history. It's her special secret! *Courtesy of Australia Zoo*

(right) An indignant Harriet is rescued by David Fleay and his young helpers. *Courtesy of Dr David Fleay Trustees*

Harriet the Galápagos giant tortoise: at a glance

CLASS
Reptilia (reptile)

GENUS
Geochelone (means 'earth tortoise')

SPECIES
nigra

SUBSPECIES
porteri

SCIENTIFIC NAME IN FULL
Geochelone nigra porteri

Harriet, at 149 years of age, meets a young admirer. *Courtesy of* Australasian Post, *6 December 1979*

PLACE OF ORIGIN

It seems likely that Harriet came from James Island (also known as Isla Santiago). Alternatively, she may have come from the island of Santa Cruz (also called Indefatigable Island). These two islands are located very close to one another, and are part of the Galápagos Island group off the coast of Ecuador in the Pacific Ocean.

In the 1800s, tortoise meat was an important food source. It was also useful as a product to sell, especially to ships sailing through the area. Young tortoises were taken from Santa Cruz to James Island, where there was a salt mine, as well as more water and vegetation for the tortoises to eat. Therefore, Harriet may have hatched on Santa Cruz, then been taken to James Island where she was picked up by Charles Darwin.

In any case, scientists say it's almost impossible to find significant differences between the two subspecies.

LIFESPAN

We hope that Harriet will reach her 200th birthday – and live for many years after that! Already, at 175 years of age, she's the oldest known living creature on Earth. According to the *Guinness Book of World Records*, Harriet will need to be over 193 years old to beat the record of the oldest living animal ever recorded. Galápagos giant tortoises are thought to be the longest living vertebrates on Earth.

CALCULATING HARRIET'S AGE

An easy way to calculate Harriet's age is to add 170 (the difference between 1830 and the year 2000) to the current year of this century. For example, in 2005 her age is 175. In 2030, Harriet will be 200 years old, with two centuries of living behind her.

SIZE

Her shell measures about one square metre. Galápagos giant tortoises are the largest tortoises in the world.

WEIGHT

Harriet weighs about 180 kilograms. Males are bigger and heavier, and can weigh over 227 kilograms.

TEMPERAMENT

Normally quiet and peaceful, Harriet's a true gentle giant. She's affectionate to her keepers. Harriet prefers human company to that of other tortoises. She will hiss or grunt if frightened. During summer Harriet spends a lot of time snoozing in her pond.

DIET

Galápagos giant tortoises are one hundred per cent vegetarian. In the wild, Harriet would have eaten a wide variety of leaves, grasses, stems, flowers and fruits – including the fruits and fleshy pads of cacti. In captivity, Harriet's daily meal – which she eats late morning – consists of a wide variety of fruits and vegetables. She also grazes on fresh grass. Giant tortoises don't chew their food, they grind it slowly into a pulp, then swallow.

FAVOURITE FOOD

Hibiscus flowers.

SHELL

A hard horny, dome-shaped shell encloses Harriet's body. The top of the shell, also called a carapace, is made up of fused bone (ribs, backbone and shoulder bones) covered with hard dry plates of skin. The shell protects the tortoise from climatic extremes and predators.

Eating her greens keeps Harriet fit and healthy. But she'd much rather have a hibiscus flower! *Courtesy of Australia Zoo*

HEAD

Harriet has a small head set on a wrinkled neck. She has no teeth. Her strong jaws are lined with sharp ridges that form a horny beak with excellent cutting edges. Eyelids protect her small, bright, inquisitive eyes.

LEGS

Harriet has four stumpy legs covered with small horny scales. Each foot is equipped with five short blunt claws.

Nothing escapes Harriet's attention. Her eyes follow you, wherever you go. *Courtesy of Queensland Newspapers Pty. Ltd.*

Comparing Tom, Dick and Harry/Harriet

ISLAND OF ORIGIN

Tom: Chatham Island (also called Isla San Cristóbal)

Dick: Charles Island (also called Santa Floreana)

Harry/Harriet: James Island (also called Santiago) or Indefatigable Island (also called Santa Cruz)

SCIENTIFIC NAME

Tom: *Geochelone nigra cathamensis* Dick: *Geochelone nigra nigra* Harry/Harriet: *Geochelone nigra darwini* or *Geochelone nigra porteri*

SEX

Tom: Unknown Dick: Female Harry/Harriet: Female

A living
link with
history

When you attach a famous name to an animal, its life can be plotted fairly accurately. Harriet's name is linked to many famous people and places. Charles Darwin and the *Beagle* voyage provide an important start. Then we can follow her life through Captain John Wickham, Brisbane Botanic Gardens, Dr David Fleay, then Australia Zoo. With every new place, Harriet makes new friends, whether they be birds, animals or people. Her life is a rich tapestry of adventure.

Although some of Harriet's records between the years 1842 and 1893 were destroyed by the Brisbane River Floods of 1893, Harriet's time-line can be traced fairly accurately. The reason is simple. Throughout the second half of the 1800s, there weren't any other tortoises like her in Australia.

HARRIET'S TIMELINE

1830

On 15 November, Harriet hatched from an egg on an island in the Galápagos Island group.

1835

She was one of three tortoises captured by Charles Darwin, for the purpose of scientific research. The trio was loaded aboard *HMS Beagle*, under the command of Captain FitzRoy. They were named Tom, Dick and Harry. Each came from a different Galápagos Island and measured about 28 centimetres in length.

1836

The *Beagle* arrived in London. Charles Darwin kept the three giant tortoises in his home and studied them for six years.

1842 (early)

Darwin decided that the cold, wet climate of England was unsuitable for Galápagos giant tortoises, so he arranged for Captain John Wickham to take the three tortoises to Australia aboard a sailing ship.

1842 (late)

The giant tortoises arrived in Queensland, Australia. They lived with John Wickham in Brisbane, moving with him from house to house. They even lived in the Governor's House!

1859

Charles Darwin published his book *On the Origin of Species by Means of Natural Selection* (usually referred to as *The Origin of Species*), which immediately became a bestseller, as well as the centre of a raging controversy.

1860

The three giant tortoises were donated to the Brisbane Botanic and Zoological Gardens. At 30 years of age Tom, Dick and Harry reached sexual maturity.

1882

Charles Darwin died at the age of 73 years. Tom, Dick and Harry turned 52 in that same year.

1890s

Dick died.

Tom enjoyed living in the Brisbane Botanic Gardens. He died at 97 years of age.
Courtesy of Professor Robin Cooke and Queensland Museum Collection

1893

A disastrous flood of the Brisbane River destroyed many irreplaceable records, including some documents about the giant tortoises.

1927

Tom died. His remains were preserved; they are currently stored in the Queensland Museum.

1939

David Fleay began studying Harry.

1958

The zoological section of the Brisbane Botanic Gardens closed. Harry was transferred to David Fleay's Fauna Reserve.

1960s

David Fleay discovered that Harry is a female! Her name was changed to Harriet.

1987

Harriet moved to Australia Zoo where it's hoped she'll spend the rest of her life.

1993

David Fleay died.

15 November: of every year

Harriet's birthday is celebrated every year at Australia Zoo. Local school children, tourists and staff give Harriet a birthday cake, flowers and plenty of attention.

Darwin's controversial book

In 1859, the same year the tortoise trio turned 29 years of age, Charles Darwin's book *The Origin of Species* was published in London. Undoubtedly, this book is one of the most important biological works ever written. It is also one of the most controversial.

Charles Darwin put forward his theory of evolution through natural selection, thereby challenging the religious belief that God creates all things. For this reason criticism, anger and hostility were directed at Darwin, especially from the church.

However, *The Origin of Species* became a bestseller all over the world, and is still in print today.

TOM, DICK AND HARRY
AND THE THEORY OF EVOLUTION

Ever since 1835, when the *Beagle* dropped anchor at the
Galápagos Islands, Darwin couldn't get Galápagos giant tortoises
out of his mind. After all, he'd ridden them like horses, he'd
eaten their flesh and he'd studied their appearance and behaviour.
And of course, he'd collected Tom, Dick and Harry, taken them
aboard the *Beagle* and carried them back home to England.
Undoubtedly, Tom, Dick and Harry helped Darwin formulate
his radical theory of evolution through natural selection.

When applied to Galápagos giant tortoises, Charles
Darwin's theory suggests that South American giant tortoises
floated to the Galápagos Islands several million years ago on
rafts of vegetation or logs. On the Galápagos Islands, where
each island was isolated from others in the group, 15 different
types (subspecies) of giant tortoises evolved. Over an immense
period of time, the South American giant tortoises changed into
today's Galápagos giant tortoises.

Darwin explained it like this. The shell shape of the tortoise –
either domed or saddle-shaped – varied according to the plant
life of the island. The markings, length of legs and length of
neck varied too. For instance, if giant tortoises had to reach up
high to feed on giant cacti, then there was an advantage for
those with a shell that curved upwards, at the front, in the

shape of a Spanish saddle. Those with long, elephant-like legs also had an advantage.

On the other hand, tortoises living in the highlands – where the grass was lush, and low-growing vegetation plentiful – evolved low-slung, domed shells that fitted snugly behind the neck, along with short necks and legs.

The giant tortoise is a live prehistoric creature: a living fossil that has outlived the dinosaurs.

Darwin further argued that Galápagos giant tortoises bred many more offspring than could survive. Not all the young giant tortoises were the same. There were many slight differences. In the struggle to survive, the giant tortoises that were best suited to their environment survived and bred the most offspring. Those that could not adapt, died out. Nature did the choosing. Natural selection took place. It was a case of the 'survival of the fittest'.

THE CHURCH DISAGREES

According to the church, God created every living thing on Earth during the six-day period of Creation described in the Book of Genesis. God created every plant and animal on Earth to suit the environment of that particular place. For instance, God created different types of Galápagos giant tortoise, each type created to suit its own particular environment.

DIFFERENT ISLANDS: DIFFERENT TORTOISES

Nobody argued, though, that there used to be 15 different types (subspecies) of Galápagos giant tortoise. Only 11 of these exist today. Many of these are endangered. Ten of these types lived on ten different islands; the other five lived on Isabela. On Isabela, each type lived in a separate volcanic crater with its small yet distinct ecosystem, separated from other types of tortoise by barren fields of lava.

IS IT NECESSARY TO TAKE SIDES?

When thinking about the differences between Darwin's theory and the story of Creation, it's helpful to remember that Darwin's theory of evolution through natural selection is backed up by many scientific facts and measurements. Fossils show part of this evidence. There is not absolute proof, however, that evolution by means of natural selection is the complete answer to the origins of life on Earth.

The story of Creation, on the other hand, centres around the Bible – with many religions believing the exact words as they were written – as the word of God. It's a matter of spiritual belief and faith.

These days, most scientists and many religious denominations accept Darwin's theory. Other people, though, think there's no need to take sides. They believe that God created the initial spark of life on Earth, and then all species evolved according to Darwin's theory of evolution through natural selection. A process that continues to this day.

Debate on this complex subject will continue well into the future. Whether you believe in Darwin's theory or the story of Creation – or a blend of both – is entirely up to you. Therefore, feel comfortable with your conclusion, no matter what it might be. The only thing that's certain is that Harriet is not the slightest bit interested in arguing about her origins, let alone the origins of life on Earth!

David Fleay's promise is kept. His great-grandchildren, Matthew and Bridget, regularly visit Harriet at Australia Zoo. *Courtesy of Angela Fleay*

Breeding Galápagos giant tortoises

DIFFERENCES BETWEEN SEXES

Males are more than 1.2 metres long and can be heavier than three men. The females are smaller. The male has a thicker, longer tail and is more hollowed out beneath its shell.

MATING

Galápagos giant tortoises mate while wallowing in muddy pools. Males utter hoarse groans and bellows, which can be heard far away.

EGGS

Females walk down to the lowlands where the sandy soil is soft for nesting. They lay their eggs at night. Each female digs a shallow hole, then lays up to 20 leathery-shelled eggs, each about the size and shape of a tennis ball. She covers her eggs with a type of 'concrete'; a mixture of damp soil and urine that bakes in the sun to form a hard lid. The nesting site is usually away from the feeding area.

INCUBATION

It takes about six months for the eggs to hatch. The sex of the hatchlings is determined by the temperature within the nest. Low temperatures produce more males, whereas high temperatures produce more females.

HATCHLINGS

Hatchlings, using their claws and a structure called an egg tooth, break out of their egg shells, then through the hard lid protecting the nest. They are independent, and measure about 7 centimetres long. They make a tasty meal for birds of prey, as well as for rats, feral pigs, dogs and cats.

SEXUAL MATURITY

At about 30 years of age Galápagos giant tortoises are mature enough to breed.

The Galápagos Islands

LOCATED ON THE EQUATOR

Situated in the Pacific Ocean, almost 1000 kilometres from the South American mainland, the Galápagos Islands are located on the equator. They belong to Ecuador, a country in South America.

UNDERWATER VOLCANOES

Formed millions of years ago by underwater volcanoes that rose from the ocean floor, these remote, rocky islands form a group of 13 or so larger islands, six smaller islets and lots of tiny islets – mostly in sight of one another. Isabela is the largest, with five volcanoes. Some of the Galápagos islands still have active volcanoes, with frequent eruptions. On many of the islands there are large areas of barren black lava rock, black cones and ancient volcanic chimneys, and black beach sand.

MANY ISLANDS: A LARGE TOTAL AREA

The Galápagos Islands are about 8000 square kilometres in area. In 1959, 95 per cent of the land mass was declared a National Park. The aim was to preserve the unique habitat for all the plants and animals living on the Galápagos Islands.

GALÁPAGO MEANS 'SADDLE'

The giant tortoises that live on the Galápagos Islands are responsible for their name. *Galápago* is the Spanish word for saddle, which describes the shape of the shells of some giant tortoise subspecies living in the Galápagos Islands.

ONLY IN THE GALÁPAGOS ISLANDS

Plant and animal life began to evolve on the Galápagos Islands several million years ago. Because it's so isolated, many of the species can be found nowhere else on Earth.

There are over 300 plant and animal species unique to the Galápagos Islands, including spiky tree-like cacti that grow to 11 metres or more, dry thorny scrub, misty forests, giant tortoises, marine iguanas, seabirds with blue feet, cormorants with shrivelled wings, and sea lions – just to mention a few of the species that are indigenous to the islands.

HITCHING A RIDE FROM SOUTH AMERICA

Yet the plants and animals of the Galápagos are similar to plants and animals native to the South American mainland. Cactus seeds, plant spores and insects were probably carried in the wind, or in ocean currents, or by seabirds (in their droppings or in mud picked up on their feet) from South America. It's also believed that a few South American finches were blown out to sea. Many millions of years ago, the ancestors of giant tortoises are thought to have hitched a ride from South America on rafts of floating vegetation or logs – crossing 1000 kilometres of open ocean.

DARWIN MADE THE GALÁPAGOS ISLANDS FAMOUS

Charles Darwin made the Galápagos Islands famous. He visited the islands for 35 days between 15 September and 20 October 1835. As he collected his specimens and observed the unique geology, marine life and land plants and animals of the islands, many questions began to form in his mind. These ultimately led to the publication of *The Origin of Species*.

THE CHARLES DARWIN FOUNDATION AND RESEARCH STATION

Scientists from all over the world come to the Galápagos Islands to build on the knowledge laid down by Charles Darwin.

In 1959 (the 100th anniversary of the publication of *The Origin of Species*), the Charles Darwin Foundation (CDF) was established and the Galápagos Island National Park was declared.

The CDF advises the Ecuadorian government on conservation issues relating to the Galápagos Islands. It also organises educational programs and raises money for research and conservation.

Harriet's elephant-like legs are covered by an armour of rough scales. *Courtesy of Australia Zoo*

The CDF also operates the Charles Darwin Research Station (CDRS) located on Santa Cruz Island. The CDRS is an international organisation established in 1964. Its main role is scientific research relating to the Galápagos Islands. Combining wildlife management, scientific research, education and the control of introduced animals and plants, the CDRS has initiated many very successful conservation programs.

The CDRS is staffed by a team of dedicated and enthusiastic

scientists (including evolutionary biologists), who come to investigate the rich diversity of life in and around the Galápagos Islands. The scientists study insects, birds, reptiles, plant and marine life, and are still discovering new species living on these islands, and in their surrounding waters.

THE SERIOUS THREAT OF FERAL ANIMALS

When pirates, whalers and explorers started visiting and settling on the Galápagos Islands centuries ago, rats, mice, dogs, cats, goats, pigs, cattle, donkeys and horses were brought in. Over the years, these animals have gone wild and threaten the unique Galápagos environment because Galápagos Island species have no natural defences against people or the animals we have introduced.

During the 1800s and 1900s, humans killed over 100,000 giant tortoises – for their meat and high quality oil.

Wild pigs, goats and rats are a serious threat to iguanas, giant tortoises and many native bird species. Even in Charles Darwin's time, rats, cats, domestic pigs and goats were a problem. Feral pigs uproot the nests of giant tortoises and land and marine iguanas, then eat their eggs and hatchlings. Cattle, donkeys and horses accidentally trample nests and eggs. Feral dogs kill fur seals, penguins and land iguanas. Rats break open giant tortoise eggs then suck clean the insides. They also eat hatchlings.

Goats strip vegetation that evolved to be eaten by giant tortoises alone. They ringbark trees that the giant tortoises need for shade. They trample water holes and use up scarce water. They also create desert-like conditions through over-grazing. In 1996, on the largest island – Isabela – there was a population of 80,000 to 100,000 wild goats! Teams of New Zealand hunters were hired to shoot them. Land iguanas and giant tortoises cannot compete with goats. On the tiny island of Pinta, 26,000 goats were shot in one year alone.

In 1835, Charles Darwin hitched a ride on a giant tortoise. During the early 1970s, riding Harriet was considered a privilege. *Courtesy of Dr David Fleay Trustees*

SAVING GIANT TORTOISES
THROUGH CAPTIVE BREEDING

The CDRS has put in place captive breeding programs to ensure the survival of giant tortoises. Within the giant tortoise hatchery and reserve, eggs (that are collected from natural nests) are incubated in special boxes. The hatchlings are then cared for in captivity until they are five years of age. Once their shells are hard enough to prevent rats and pigs eating them, they are released back into their natural environment. Sometimes the hatchlings are released earlier if their island is free of rats, feral dogs and wild pigs. Once the tortoises have reached sexual maturity, they breed naturally and re-populate their particular island with its unique subspecies.

In 1972, a group of shooters who were culling goats on the volcanic island of Pinta discovered a lone giant tortoise hiding in the highlands. This was a very important discovery because Pinta giant tortoises were thought to be extinct. They named him Lonesome George. He is the only known remaining giant tortoise of his subspecies. He's over 80 years old, has a saddle-shaped shell and currently lives in a captive breeding enclosure with female giant tortoises of a similar subspecies, from the island of Española. So far there have been no baby tortoises.

Has Lonesome George's subspecies evolved into a new species, only to face extinction? An international search is underway to find a female of the same subspecies, to save the Pinta Island tortoises from dying out forever. But time is running out. If Lonesome George dies without producing young, there will be only ten of the original 15 subspecies of Galápagos giant tortoises left in the world. The Pinta subspecies will become extinct. Giant tortoises have lived on the island of Pinta for at least one million years.

Other captive breeding programs have been extraordinarily successful. On the island of Española, the number of giant tortoises dropped to as few as 14 (two males and 12 females) in 1968. This subspecies, with its very long neck and exaggerated saddle-shaped shell, was on the brink of extinction. As a result of the captive breeding program there are now about 1000 of these tortoises living on the island of Española. The original population is estimated to have been about 3000 tortoises.

However, because these 1000 tortoises have been bred from so few individuals, there is a serious lack of diversity of the special characteristics that are passed on from parents to their young. Consequently, the Española subspecies of giant tortoise is still at risk. Disease, or any large change within their environment, could kill off most of these tortoises and once again place the subspecies in danger of extinction.

Glossary

Aldabra giant tortoises
A species of giant tortoise native to Aldabra Island, situated off the east coast of Africa, just a little to the north of Madagascar, in the Indian Ocean.

ancient
Existing in the earliest times.

breed (reproduction)
To produce young.

browse
To eat the leaves and branches of trees and shrubs, as well as different types of grasses.

camouflage
A type of disguise in the form of colours and patterns which blend into the background and make an animal or plant difficult to see against its surroundings.

carapace
The top of a tortoise's shell, formed from overgrown, widened ribs and covered with horny plates.

classify
Arrange in an order that shows differences as well as similarities.

cold blooded
Unable to control their body temperature, which means their temperature is the same as the temperature of the surrounding air or water. For this reason these animals are usually found in warm places.

Creationism
The belief that everything existing on Earth today was created directly by God, during the six-day period of Creation – described in the Bible, in the Book of Genesis.

diarrhoea
Runny droppings.

digest
To break down food so it is able to be absorbed by the body.

ecosystem
All the living things within an environment and the way in which they relate to one another and to their environment.

endangered
In danger of dying out.

environment
All the elements of a place, including the land, weather, water, plants and animals.

equator
The imaginary circle around the middle of the Earth, halfway between the North Pole and South Pole. The climate is usually hot.

evolution
The scientific theory that all plant and animal species have developed from earlier forms – usually by gradual genetic change, over long periods of time – by means of natural selection. New species are formed this way. Evolution suggests that all living things form part of the single web of life.

extinction
The disappearance of an entire species. If an animal species is extinct, this means there is not a single living animal of that kind anywhere in the world.

feral
A domesticated animal that has become wild.

fertile (reproduction)
Able to produce young of their own.

fossils
The remains (or imprints) of animals or plants from long ago, preserved in layers of rock, or in amber (fossilised sap from ancient trees and plants).

geographic isolation
An environment that is separate. For example, a small island.

geology
The scientific study of all the rocks that form the Earth's crust.

hatchling
An animal newly hatched from an egg.

hibernate
To spend the winter in a dormant (sleepy) state – usually hidden away.

incubate

To keep eggs at a particular temperature (naturally or artificially) while they are developing to the hatching stage.

introduced

A plant or animal brought into an environment from somewhere else. An introduced animal or plant can take over the habitat from native species. For example, European rabbits introduced into Australia have taken over the habitat of native animals such as bilbies.

lava

Hot liquid rock that flows from an erupting volcano. When cool, this forms rock.

mate

When males and females of the same species join together to produce offspring.

molten

Made into a liquid by heat.

native

An animal or plant belonging to a particular environment.

naturalist

A person who studies nature, as a science.

natural selection

Charles Darwin's theory that those individuals best suited to survive in a particular environment are more likely to breed, and so pass on their desirable characteristics to their offspring – also called 'survival of the fittest'. This is the central idea of evolution, whereby species change in time.

offspring

The young of a particular animal.

organisms

Living things.

plankton

Animals and plants which drift or float in the ocean, in huge numbers. They vary in size from microscopic organisms to jellyfish.

quarantine

The isolating of animals (or people) for a period of time to make sure they don't spread disease.

reptile

An animal with a backbone, that has scaly skin and whose body temperature changes as the surrounding air or water temperature changes. Reptiles may live on land or in the water, but all breathe air, using lungs. They usually lay soft-shelled eggs.

sexual maturity
Old enough to breed young of their own.

species
A group of similar animals or plants which breed with each other (to produce fertile offspring), but will not breed with members of any other species.

specimens
Single things collected as being typical of a whole group of things. For example, a collection of beetle specimens.

subspecies
A group of similar animals or plants that are different (in colour, size or shape) to others of its species, but can still reproduce within the species. A subspecies usually lives in geographic isolation (for instance, on an island) from others of its species. Darwin's theory of evolution through natural selection suggests that when a subspecies changes to the degree that it's unable to breed within its species, it is considered a new species. So, subspecies can change (evolve) into new species. As living things are continually evolving, sometimes it's difficult to know whether or not an animal is a species or subspecies. This is evolution at work.

theory
In science, an idea or explanation based on observation and reason.

tropical
Located near the equator.

vegetarian
Eats only plant food.

vertebrate
An animal that possesses a bony skeleton (usually with a backbone protecting its spinal cord and a skull protecting its brain) and a well-developed brain.

volcano
A mountain, usually with an opening at the top, out of which molten rock, ash and steam spout when it is active.

wildlife
Animals, birds, insects and plants living together in their natural surroundings.

zoologist
A person who studies animal life, as a science.

Further Reading

No other scientist has caught the attention of as many writers as Charles Darwin. As a result, you'll find countless books about him. The Galápagos Islands are also a popular topic. The following books and internet addresses are a good place to start.

Blashfield, Jean. *Wonders of the World: Galápagos Islands*. Raintree Steck-Vaughn, United States, 1995.

Chambers, Paul. *A Sheltered Life: The Unexpected History of the Giant Tortoise*. John Murray, London, 2004.

Darwin, Charles. *Beagle Diary*. Cambridge University Press, United Kingdom, 1988.

Darwin, Charles. *The Illustrated Origin of Species (Abridged and Introduced by Richard Leakey)*. Oxford University Press, London, 1979.

Darwin, Charles. *On the Origin of Species*. J. M. Dent and Sons Ltd, London, 1928.

Darwin, Charles. *Voyage of the Beagle*. Penguin Books, London, 1989.

Darwin, Francis. *The Life of Charles Darwin*. John Murray, London, 1902.

Fleay, David. *Looking at Animals with David Fleay*. Boolarong Publications, Australia, 1981.

Fullick, Ann. *Charles Darwin*. Heinemann Library, United Kingdom, 2000.

Gamlin, Linda. *Evolution*. Dorling Kindersley, United Kingdom, 1993.

Keynes, Richard. *Charles Darwin in Australia*. Cambridge University Press, United Kingdom, 2002.

Moorehouse, Alan. *Darwin and the Beagle*. Hamish Hamilton, London, 1969.

Myerson, George. *Darwin's Origin of Species: A Beginner's Guide*. Hodder & Stoughton, United Kingdom, 2001.

Parker, Steve. *Charles Darwin and Evolution*. Belitha Press, United Kingdom, 1992.

Ralling, Christopher. *The Voyage of Charles Darwin*. British Broadcasting Corp., London, United Kingdom, 1978.

Sproule, Anna. *Charles Darwin*. Exley Publications, United Kingdom, 1990.

Stewart, Robin. *Charles Darwin's Big Idea*. Hyland House, Australia, 2005.

Strathern, Paul. *Darwin and Evolution*. Arrow Books, United Kingdom, 1998.

Tagliaferro, Victor. *Galápagos Islands: Nature's Delicate Balance at Risk*. Lerner Publications, USA, 2001.

Torr Patrick. *Charles Darwin: The Scholar who Changed Human History*. Thames & Hudson, United Kingdom, 2001.

Whitfield, Philip. *Evolution: The Greatest Story Ever Told*. Marshall Publishing, United Kingdom, 1998.

Whitfield, Philip. *The Natural History of Evolution*. Doubleday, United Kingdom, 1993.

You can 'visit' the Natural History Museum in London, and view special exhibitions on Darwin, as well as a fantastic display of the many species on Earth at www.nhm.ac.uk

Interesting information about the Galápagos Islands can be found at: www.darwinfoundation.org www.Galapagos.org

By doing a Google search on Galápagos giant tortoises you'll find many interesting sites.

Acknowledgments

Since childhood I've read everything about the natural world I could lay my hands on. Therefore, my sincere thanks go to all the authors who gave me the gift of their knowledge and understanding.

My husband Doug has given me his whole-hearted support throughout the process of meeting Harriet, researching her story and creating this book. I thank his generosity of spirit, most sincerely.

A special thank you to the entire team at Black Inc. who are always such a pleasure to work with. Sincere thanks to Morry Schwartz, Sophy Williams, Nadine Davidoff and Anna Lensky for believing in this book and sharing my passion for Harriet.

Thank you to Rosemary Fleay-Thomson (Dr David Fleay's daughter and author of the biography, *Animals First*) for giving me delightful insights into Harriet's life with the Fleay family in Queensland; Angela Fleay (Dr David Fleay's grand-daughter) and Matthew and Bridget (his great-grandchildren); Kerri Hall, Librarian, Australian History and Literature Team, State Library of Victoria; David Gibson, Director, Newstead House, Queensland; Lynn Meyers, Reference Librarian, John Oxley Library, Queensland; Patricia Parr, Reproduction Rights Officer, Heritage Collections, State Library of Queensland; Heather Richards, Historian, Brisbane City Council, Queensland; Michelle at the Brisbane *Courier-Mail*; Patrick Couper, Queensland Museum; Janice Wilson, Director, Queensland Museum Foundation; Professor Robin Cooke who shares my keen interest in Harriet; and Michael Gatehouse for reading the manuscript and making valuable suggestions.

Photo credits
Australia Zoo
Brisbane *Courier-Mail*
Collection: John Oxley Library
State Library of Queensland – Negative
    Number 52622
Dr David Fleay Trustees
Doug Stewart
Professor Robin Cooke
Janice Wilson (Director), Queensland
    Museum Collection.

Index